DATE DUE

SEP 0 7 2006	
SEP 2 0 2006	
DEC 0 5 2006	
APR 0 2 2007	
APR 1 3 2007	
APR 2 7 2007	
SEP 0 7 2016	
SEP 2 1 2016	

Violence in the Media

Look for these and other books in the Lucent Overview Series:

Abortion
Acid Rain
Adoption
AIDS
Bigotry
Cancer
Censorship
Cities
Civil Liberties
Cloning
Cults
The Death Penalty
Divorce
DNA on Trial
Drug Abuse
Drugs and Sports
Drug Trafficking
Eating Disorders
Endangered Species
Environmental Groups
Epidemics
Ethnic Violence
Euthanasia
Family Violence
Gambling
Gangs
Gay Rights
Global Resources
Gun Control
Hazardous Waste
Health Care

Homeless Children
Human Rights
Illegal Immigration
The Internet
Juvenile Crime
Medical Ethics
Mental Illness
Militias
Money
Multicultural America
Obesity
Oil Spills
The Palestinian-Israeli Accord
Paranormal Phenomena
Police Brutality
Population
Poverty
Rap Music
The Rebuilding of Bosnia
Saving the American Wilderness
Schools
School Violence
Sexual Harassment
Sports in America
Suicide
Terrorism
The U.S. Congress
The U.S. Presidency
Violence Against Women
Women's Rights
Zoos

Violence in the Media

by LeeAnne Gelletly

LUCENT
BOOKS ®

THOMSON
—★—TM
GALE

San Diego • Detroit • New York • San Francisco • Cleveland • New Haven, Conn. • Waterville, Maine • London • Munich

© 2005 by Lucent Books ®. Lucent Books ® is an imprint of Thomson Gale, a part of the Thomson Corporation.

Thomson is a trademark and Gale [and Lucent Books] are registered trademarks used herein under license.

For more information, contact
Lucent Books
27500 Drake Rd.
Farmington Hills, MI 48331-3535
Or you can visit our Internet site at http://www.gale.com

LIBRARY OF CONGRESS CATALOGING-IN-PUBLICATION DATA

Gelletly, LeeAnne.
   Violence in the media / by LeeAnne Gelletly.
     p. cm. — (Overview series)
Includes bibliographical references and index.
Summary: Explores the issue of violence in television, films, music, and other forms of media, with an examination of the link between media violence and real-life violence and discussion of the steps that have been taken to regulate violent media.
   ISBN 1-56006-508-7 (hard cover : alk. paper)
   1. Violence in mass media. I. Title. II. Series.
P96.V5G397 2004
303.6—dc22

                                     2004010692

Printed in the United States of America

Contents

Introduction

In DECEMBER 1997, a fourteen-year-old boy shot and killed three teenagers and wounded five others at Heath High School in West Paducah, Kentucky. In April 1999, two teenage students in Littleton, Colorado, planned to blow up Columbine High School after a shooting spree that took fifteen lives, including their own. During a three-week rampage in October 2002, a seventeen-year-old sniper and his older mentor terrorized the Washington, D.C., area, killing ten people and wounding three.

Some people believe these horrific acts occurred because violent media—movies, television shows, music, or video games—created these young killers. Psychologists and media experts theorized that Paducah resident Michael Carneal was inspired to emulate a scene from the 1995 movie *The Basketball Diaries*. The fascination of Columbine killers Eric Harris and Dylan Klebold with "shock rock" musician Marilyn Manson and the video game Doom is believed to have provoked their deadly rampage. Lawyers for sniper suspect Lee Boyd Malvo stated in his defense that the boy "obsessed" over the movie *The Matrix* and had been brainwashed into becoming a cold-blooded killer by playing ultraviolent video games.

After the March 1998 school shootings in Jonesboro, Arkansas, psychologist Dr. Stephen Garber stated that the fault for youth violence lay with the media. Garber told a CNN reporter, "What we see happening is that there is so much . . . realistic-type violence portrayed in movies and in other situations. [It affects] certain kinds of kids who can't tell the difference between reality and fantasy. They think that if you shoot somebody, they get up."[1]

Others disagree. They say that blaming entertainment violence for real-life violence is far too simplistic—other social factors such as uninvolved parenting, child abuse, neighborhood violence, and mental illness can cause people to act aggressively. However, few could disagree that violence has been around for a long time, in both the real world and human imagination.

Lawyers for teenage sniper Lee Boyd Malvo blamed his 2002 shooting spree on his obsession with the violent 1996 film The Matrix.

The attractions of violence

For centuries people have been entertained by conflict, violence, and death. From their seats in huge amphitheaters, ancient Romans cheered wild beast hunts and deadly gladiator duels. Spectators at medieval tournaments reveled in bloody jousts and other deadly reenactments of thirteenth-century warfare. Mobs thronged to public executions. Storytellers from Homer to Shakespeare captivated audiences with tales of betrayal, war, destruction, and murder.

During the nineteenth century, gory details of catastrophes, murders, and other mayhem splashed across the pages of best-selling newspapers, magazines, and dime novels. With the birth of the film industry at the turn of the twentieth century, popular movies offered images of violent gun battles, warfare, and killings. Television did the same in the 1950s, when the first TV broadcasts reached across the country. By the end of the twentieth century, people could find plenty of violence in all manner of media—movies, television, song lyrics, and computer and video games.

Why are depictions of violence popular? Some researchers believe it is because violence fulfills a basic human need. Most people like to be frightened, especially when they know they are not themselves in any real physical danger. Today's films and video games can envelope audiences and players in realistically violent environments, inducing tension and terror, a rush of adrenaline, and a thrill of relief. But, some people believe, if watching violent films or playing action-packed video games can cause such short-term emotional and physiological reactions, perhaps violent media can change people in other, longer-lasting ways.

Violent media and real-life mayhem

From the time that television first entered the lives of Americans in the 1950s, many people blamed its violent content for the rising number of assaults, murders, and suicides among youth in American society. When arrests of young people for serious violent offenses surged by 70 percent from 1983 to 1993, and homicides tripled over the same period, public interest groups pointed a finger at increasingly violent TV programs, movies, and video games.

Although arrest and homicide rates began to decline after the mid-1990s, on average more than 150,000 young people continue to be arrested each year for violent crimes, more than 300,000 are seriously assaulted, and 3,500 are murdered. In fact, homicide, suicide, and trauma are the leading causes of death in children and adolescents.

Some scientists say that a world of violent media has helped create a real-life violent world. For more than fifty years, studies have claimed to show a link between the

Video footage from the cafeteria of Columbine High School shows Dylan Klebold and Eric Harris during their murderous 1999 rampage. The teenagers had practiced the attack by reprogramming the video game Doom II to depict the corridors of their school.

viewing of violent programs, films, and games and emotional damage and behavioral changes, particularly in young people.

Others dispute such claims. Author Gerard Jones says that viewing violence causes no harm. He believes that violence, particularly fantasy violence, is a necessary part of growing up. In his book *Killing Monsters: Why Children Need Fantasy, Super Heroes, and Make-Believe Violence*, he argues that fantasy violence helps children explore their angers and fears through playacting. "Play, fantasy, and emotional imagination are essential tools of the work of childhood and adolescence,"[2] he says. By dealing with violence, children learn to deal with fear and ultimately feel safer, Jones maintains.

An ongoing controversy

As controversy has simmered over whether or not media violence causes real-life violence, politicians and other advocacy groups have pressed for legislation to regulate the entertainment industry. Such attempts have been met by outcries of censorship, along with claims that any kind of government restriction runs counter to freedom of expression, a First Amendment right guaranteed by the U.S. Constitution. However, threats of government regulation and pressures from public interest groups have resulted in the creation of self-regulatory codes within the television, film, music, and video game industries. The effectiveness of these ratings systems is much debated.

Meanwhile, the controversy over violent media content continues unabated, with social scientists and scholars, politicians and private citizens weighing in on the issue. In 2000 President Bill Clinton offered his views, pointing out that the media exert a powerful influence and urging entertainment industry leaders to show more responsibility in how they portray violence. "This is in some ways the newest of issues, in some ways the oldest,"[3] he stated, noting that violence in entertainment was a concern as far back as the time of the ancient Greek philosopher Plato.

1

Violence in Film and Television

MORE THAN A century has passed since an eager audience crowded into Koster & Bial's Music Hall in New York City and beheld an astonishing new invention. The April 23, 1896, demonstration of Edison's Vitascope marked the first time motion pictures had been projected onto a screen for a paying audience in the United States. The pioneering moviegoers were treated to a short black-and-white sequence showing ballet dancers. While a two- or three-minute silent film presenting a snippet of ordinary life would hardly hold the attention of today's sophisticated film fans, to people who had never seen moving images, the effect was stunning. And from such humble beginnings would grow a huge and lucrative entertainment industry.

Violence in early film

Inspired to use the new medium to tell a story, director and cameraman Edwin S. Porter put together an eleven-minute silent film called *The Great Train Robbery* in 1903. The first Western, the movie relied on violence in its drama—a story of theft, pursuit, and capture. *The Great Train Robbery* featured a beating victim (obviously a dummy) who was thrown from a moving train, and actors who stumbled and fell when shot, although they had no visible wounds. Still, the novelty of film shocked and frightened early movie viewers, who actually ducked when a pistol was fired in their direction.

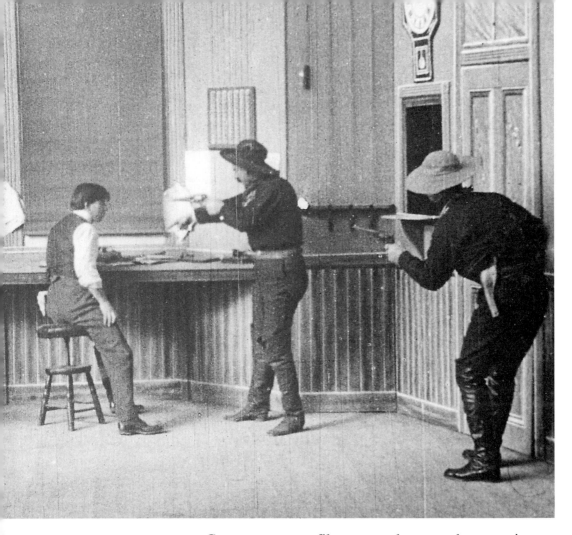

Violence was a part of the earliest films, as this holdup scene from The Great Train Robbery *(1903) indicates.*

Controversy over film content began at the same time as the technology's invention, although the first outcry came over the showing of a kiss. Soon municipal and state governments set up film censorship boards to review movies and prevent the showing of any considered objectionable to their citizens.

In 1922 several movie studios banded together to form a trade association. They called themselves the Motion Picture Producers and Distributors of America (MPPDA), later renamed the Motion Picture Association of America (MPAA). The new film association decided to deal with potential censorship of films by eliminating offensive material during the making, or production, of the film. Directors had to follow certain rules outlined in the Production Code, or the Hays Code (after MPPDA president William H. Hays).

A special office called the Production Code Administration (PCA) reviewed scripts to ensure that movies avoided controversial subjects, language, and behavior. Nudity, profanity, and ridicule of religion were banned. Illegal or immoral acts were not to be portrayed in sympathetic ways, and violence could be implied but not depicted realistically. Depiction of illegal drug use or of brutal killings could not be shown on-screen or glamorized in ways that might inspire imitation.

Sanitized violence

Because the major film studios would not distribute any movie that did not receive the PCA seal of approval, "sanitized violence" became the norm for most story lines involving conflict. As a result, as Stephen Prince explains in the introduction to his book *Screening Violence*, "in countless

William H. Hays (standing, center) watches as PCA censors review movie scripts. The censors deleted dialogue and scenes that were not considered appropriate.

Westerns and urban crime dramas, shooting victims frowned and sank gracefully out of frame, with their white shirts immaculate."[4]

Audiences flocked to violent crime dramas, such as *The Public Enemy* (1931) and *Scarface* (1932), featuring vicious heroes and cold-blooded killings. But the deaths were muted by the Production Code. For example, explains film studies professor Thomas Doherty, in the 1938 film *Angels with Dirty Faces*, "James Cagney is dragged off to the electric chair—you see the lights dim and you see maybe the shadow of the guard throwing the switch, but you certainly never see Cagney in the chair [being electrocuted]."[5]

Violence was also muted in the first horror films, which were released around the same time. Deaths occurred in the 1931 films *Dracula* and *Frankenstein*, but they happened offscreen.

Pushing the envelope

From the 1930s to the 1950s, the PCA monitored the production of all films, ensuring that controversial elements were removed from scripts. But in the 1960s, the industry's system of self-censorship was discarded. Preferring to introduce controversy in films, directors no longer abided by the Production Code. Some began experimenting with different ways to emphasize violence in order to create a greater emotional impact. They developed techniques such as multicamera filming (running more than one camera) to capture action sequences from various angles. Segments of fistfights and gun battles were depicted in slow motion to allow the camera to linger on them.

Graphic depiction of bloody gunshot wounds became possible in the 1960s with the invention of squibs—blood capsules wired to explode on cue. Multiple squibs created the horrifying image of bodies being riddled with bullets, a cinematic death featured for the first time in slow motion in Arthur Penn's 1967 film *Bonnie and Clyde*. Its sexual and shockingly violent content appealed to some viewers.

In early films violence was implied, rather than depicted on-screen. Thus viewers of the 1938 film Angels with Dirty Faces *saw James Cagney in the shadow of the electric chair but not his execution.*

Others were appalled and began to protest that the movie industry was going too far.

Creation of film ratings

In the 1960s a number of religious organizations and advocacy groups began to call for legislation to regulate the movie industry. Concerned about the possibility of future government intervention or censorship, the film industry determined that the time was right for creating its own national ratings system.

In 1968 the MPAA, the International Film Importers and Distributors of America, and the National Association of Theatre Owners announced a new self-regulatory

Bonnie and Clyde *(1967) was nominated for an Academy Award for Best Picture despite its shocking and graphic violence.*

system, based on the age of moviegoers. MPAA president Jack Valenti explained that the industry would no longer edit film content, as had been done with the Production Code. Instead, the MPAA would provide a voluntary ratings system for the use of parents: "The movie industry . . . would now see [its] primary task as giving advance cautionary warnings to parents so that parents could make the decision about the moviegoing of their young children."[6]

After revisions in 1984 and 1990, the MPAA code was established as follows: According to the MPAA website, films considered suitable for general audiences receive a G rating, indicating they contain "nothing in theme, language, nudity and sex, violence, etc. [that] would, in the view of the Rating Board, be offensive to parents whose younger children view the film."[7]

The PG rating indicates that parental guidance is suggested. Some of the movie's content might be considered unsuitable for children.

The PG-13 label identifies a film as acceptable for general audiences, but indicates that it has "a higher level of intensity" than that found in a film rated PG, although it "does not quite fit within the restricted R category."[8] The PG-13 rating came about in 1984, in response to an outcry over the release of Steven Spielberg's PG-rated *Indiana Jones and the Temple of Doom*. The violence of some of its scenes, such as one that featured a beating heart being ripped from the chest of a sacrificial victim, shocked and offended many viewers. They demanded to know why the film had not been given an R rating.

R-rated films feature "hard language, or tough violence or nudity within sensual scenes, or drug abuse or other elements."[9] Those under the age of seventeen may not gain admittance to a movie theater to view an R-rated film, unless they are accompanied by a parent or guardian.

According to the MPAA code, NC-17 (originally X) films fall into the "adults only" category. The rating describes a movie that most parents would want to bar their minor children from viewing, and no one age seventeen or younger may be admitted into a theater to see a film with the NC-17 rating.

How movie ratings are assigned

To receive a film rating, directors pay a fee and voluntarily submit their movies to an MPAA board, which is made up of eight to thirteen Los Angeles–area parents paid to review and rate individual movies. After viewing the movie, the members determine its rating by a majority vote. According to the MPAA website, the entirety of a film's content—including theme, language, nudity, sex, drug use, and violence—is considered in determining the movie's rating. And violence, the MPAA says, is just as important as the other elements is assigning a rating.

The ratings system is voluntary, and films that are not submitted to the MPAA board do not receive a rating. Such films, which are usually international or independent productions, must be advertised as unrated, which makes them more difficult to market.

Early years of the small screen

While not as old as motion pictures, television has become arguably the most influential of the mass media. Invented in the 1920s, television made its first appearance before the public at the RCA Pavilion of the 1939 World's Fair in New York City. Two years later, the Federal Communications Commission (FCC), the federal agency in charge of regulating the public airwaves, granted the first television station license. By the late 1940s and early 1950s, three main broadcasting networks were operating coast-to-coast: CBS, NBC, and ABC.

In 1951 television programs reached approximately 6 million homes, or about 9 percent of American households. By 1960 ten times as many families—about 60 million—boasted of having a television console in their living room. And by 1965 almost 93 percent of American households had at least one TV set.

Even in television's early years many people believed that the violent content of certain television programming was having a bad influence on children. TV was blamed for a rise in youth crime, or juvenile delinquency. The federal government was quick to investigate the issue, with the House Interstate and Foreign Commerce Committee holding hearings on radio and televised violence as early as 1952. Two years later, the Senate Judiciary Committee, under chairman Estes Kefauver, evaluated the role of television in its investigation of juvenile delinquency.

TV during a turbulent decade

Violence from the real world entered people's homes through television news, and the 1960s was filled with mayhem. Two days after the November 22, 1963, assassination of President John F. Kennedy, an NBC camera crew captured the murder of Kennedy's presumed assassin, Lee Harvey Oswald, on live TV. By the mid-1960s broadcasts of combat footage from the Vietnam War brought bloodshed and death into people's living rooms on a daily basis.

Images of assaults and killings during civil rights marches and antiwar protests also filled the small screen.

During the 1960s much of the violence in the real world was also being reflected in fictional television programming. Among the most popular—and violent—shows were the Western *Gunsmoke* (1955–1975) and the crime drama *The Untouchables* (1959–1963).

The federal government continued to evaluate the issue of television violence and its potential for harming children. Legislators held hearings, and President Lyndon Johnson convened the National Commission on the Causes and Prevention of Violence, headed by Milton Eisenhower. Its 1969 *Report of the National Commission on the Causes and Prevention of Violence* found a definite link between aggressive behavior and the viewing of violent television programs.

Warnings

Government-funded research on television violence also lent support to the theory that television was creating an increasingly violent society. One government-supported researcher from the University of Pennsylvania, George Gerbner, and his colleagues studied television content from 1967 to 1985. The results of his Cultural Indicators Project led Gerbner to state, "Never was a culture so filled with full-color images of violence as ours is now."[10] The researchers reported that the average child saw more than 8,000 murders and 100,000 acts of violence on television during the elementary school years.

In 1972 the report of the U.S. Surgeon General's Advisory Committee on Television and Social Behavior supported the earlier findings. It stated, "Televised violence, indeed, does have an adverse effect on certain members of our society."[11]

Many medical professionals added their voices to the warnings about television violence, calling it a significant threat to the public's health. In 1976 the American Medical Association adopted a resolution "to actively oppose TV programs containing violence, as well as products and/or services sponsoring such programs."[12] In 1982 the National

Institute of Mental Health reported on the dangers of media violence, and two years later the Attorney General's Task Force on Family Violence echoed that warning.

Throughout the 1970s and 1980s television was changing, but not in response to concerns over media violence. With the creation of additional small networks and cable and satellite networks, the industry was becoming bigger. As a result, many more programming choices became available.

Cable and broadcast network television shows were competing to attract audiences, often by featuring shows containing increasing amounts of graphic violence, sexual situations, and profanity. Two of the most controversial dramas on the broadcast networks were *Hill Street Blues* (1981–1987) and *St. Elsewhere* (1983–1988). In attempting to portray realistically the issues affecting America's inner cities, each of these award-winning shows offended many viewers. Others were disturbed that R-rated films ran unedited on cable networks like Home Box Office (HBO).

Regulating the television industry

Beginning in the 1960s several advocacy groups began lobbying the federal government to push for reforms in the television industry. Established in 1968 because of concerns about the lack of quality children's programming and the abundance of commercials, Action for Children's Television sought to apply political and legal pressure to force changes. Its members filed petitions and brought lawsuits against the television industry.

In 1975 the National Parent Teacher Association (PTA) passed a resolution demanding that the networks and local television stations cut back on the amount of violence in their programs and the number of commercials targeting children. Other public interest groups took action as well. Among these groups were the National Council for Families and Television, founded in 1977, and the National Coalition on Television Violence, established in 1980.

In 1990 Congress responded to the issue by passing the Simon-Glickman Television Violence Act, which encouraged

A policeman lies dead on the pavement in a scene from Hill Street Blues. *The TV series generated controversy because of its unsentimental presentation of police work and violent crime.*

the three major broadcast networks—NBC, CBS, and ABC—to develop a joint policy statement on violence. Congress also enacted the Children's Television Act (CTA), which called on broadcast television stations to increase the amount of educational and informational programming they offered to viewers under age sixteen. The act also limited the amount of commercial advertising that could be broadcast during programming targeted to children.

The three networks released their joint policy statement on violence in 1992 and stated their intent to hold an industry-wide leadership conference on the topic. In 1993 they were joined by a fourth new major broadcast network, Fox, in agreeing to air "parental advisories," which would warn viewers of shows that might be considered violent. Later that year fifteen major cable networks also signed on to this policy.

Still, complaints about the increasing amounts of sexual content and graphic violence in television programming continued. In 1996 the federal government took further action, passing the Telecommunications Act. The new law required broadcast and cable networks to "establish voluntary rules for rating programming that contains sexual, violent or other indecent material about which parents should be informed before it is displayed to children."[13] Despite their stated reservations, by the following year the networks complied with the requirement.

Television ratings labels

In January 1997 the National Association of Broadcasters, the National Cable Television Association, and the Motion Picture Association of America instituted a voluntary television ratings system. Known as the "TV Parental Guidelines," the ratings system initially was based only on age-appropriate categories. In response to complaints that viewers needed more information about a show's content, the industry added letter symbols: V specifies that the show will contain violence, S indicates the presence of sexual situations, L stands for language, and D indicates sexually suggestive dialogue. When applicable, the letter symbols appear with the appropriate-age category.

All television programs except news, sports, and unedited movies on premium cable channels receive the TV Parental Guidelines labels. They appear in the corner of the television screen during the first 15 seconds of each program and are usually featured in magazine and newspaper guides to television listings. Ratings are assigned by the TV Parental Guidelines Monitoring Board, which consists of twenty-four members drawn from the broadcast television industry, the cable industry, the program production community, and advocacy groups.

Television Ratings System

TV-Y
(All Children)
- Denotes shows made for children ages two to six
- Shows with this rating are appropriate for all children

TV-Y7
(Older Children)
- Denotes shows for children age seven and up
- These programs often contain "mild fantasy violence" or "comedic violence"
- The label TV-Y7-FV is used for programs in which fantasy violence may be more intense

TV-G
(General Audience)
- Suitable for all ages, but not necessarily a children's show
- Contains little or no violence, no strong language, and little or no sexual language or situations

TV-PG
(Parental Guidance Suggested)
- May be unsuitable for younger children
- This rating may include the additional labels **V** (violence), **S** (sexual situations), **L** (coarse language), or **D** (suggestive dialogue)

TV-14
(Parents Strongly Cautioned)
- Contains material that may be unsuitable for children under fourteen
- Intense objectionable content may be indicated by **V**, **S**, **L**, or **D** ratings

TV-MA
(Mature Audiences Only)
- Denotes a show designed for adults that may be unsuitable for anyone under age seventeen
- The **V**, **S**, **L**, or **D** labels would indicate graphic or explicit objectionable content

Source: Federal Communications Commission.

Complaints about the networks' lack of compliance in providing more educational programming, as required by the Children's Television Act, led the FCC to establish firmer guidelines in 1996. It issued the so-called three-hour rule, which specified the number of hours per week that broadcasters had to air programs that were educational and informational. These shows receive an E/I rating and are followed by the appropriate age of the intended audience.

The V-chip

The Telecommunications Act of 1996 also required that the television ratings system be used in conjunction with a new kind of technology called the V-chip. Invented in 1991 by Canadian engineering professor Tim Collins, the V-chip reads encoded information on the rating assigned to each television program and can be programmed to block shows based on the rating. The Telecommunications Act mandated that by the year 2000, all new televisions with screens thirteen inches or larger had to contain V-chip technology. Older sets could be fitted with the V-chip, which was available as a separate, set-top box.

A 2001 survey by the Kaiser Family Foundation suggested that the V-chip's impact was minimal, however. More than four in five parents reported concern that their children were seeing sexual and violent content, yet only 17 percent of the parents who owned a TV set with a V-chip actually used it to block inappropriate programs (and counting those who did not have a set with a V-chip, the overall rate was just 7 percent).

TV violence by the numbers

Additional research studies of television content continue to show that much of the programming is violent. Using data from one study, researcher Aletha Huston and colleagues have estimated that by the age of eighteen, the typical American youth will have witnessed more than 200,000 violent acts, including 40,000 murders, on television alone.

In 1994 researchers began a major three-year study of television violence. Funded by the Cable Television Association in the United States, the National Television Violence Study (NTVS) examined the amount of violence shown on 2,500 hours of programming during the 1994 through 1997 viewing seasons. The NTVS randomly sampled programs from 6:00 A.M. to 11:00 P.M. on twenty-three broadcast and cable channels from October to June.

The NTVS defined three primary types of violent depictions: credible threats, behavior acts, and harmful consequences. The report indicated that 61 percent of programs contained violence, with most of it portrayed in a glamorized way. Only 4 percent of the programs featured an anti-violence theme. Cable programs, usually showing movies, featured the highest percentage of violence. Children's programming, which included Saturday morning and after-school cartoons, contained 10 percent more violence than did adult shows. In fact, most of the nearly two-thirds of violent programming was found in children's television shows.

Of all the violent episodes studied, 58 percent were depicted without any indication of victim pain, 47 percent showed no evidence of harm to the victim, and 40 percent depicted harm, but unrealistically. Of all violent scenes on television, 86 percent featured no blood or gore. And only 16 percent showed long-term, realistic consequences of violence. In 40 percent of the cases, the program's hero initiated the violence. "These patterns teach children that violence is desirable, necessary, and painless,"[14] said Dr. Dale Kunkel, a senior researcher for the study.

The National Television Violence Study also reported that approximately 75 percent of television programs identified as violent featured characters who hurt or killed others without any punishment or negative consequences. Researchers were most concerned that the television programs seldom showed the harmful consequences of violence. Based on the data gathered, researchers concluded that TV violence posed a serious risk to children, because it encouraged aggressive behavior without regard to consequences.

Over the course of the three-year study, NTVS researchers had noted a rise in the amount of violence featured in prime-time broadcasting and on cable shows. A study released in 2003 by the Parents Television Council (PTC) shows that the amount of violence has continued to increase. The PTC counted the number of violent incidents that occurred during prime time on the six major broadcast networks (ABC, NBC, CBS, Fox, WB, and UPN) in November 1998 and in November 2002. In 1998 researchers identified 292 violent incidents on television broadcasts; four years later that number had jumped to 534. PTC president Brent Bozell told the Associated Press, "In both quantity and quality, it is getting worse. I think it is a cause for concern."[15]

Graphic images

The technology to depict violence realistically did not exist in the early days of film and television. Black-and-white images gave way to color in film during the late 1940s, and in television in the 1960s. Bloody wounds became red and gory, particularly when caused by multiple-squibs "gunfire." With advancements in the use of plastics and latex during the 1970s and 1980s, special-effects artists sculpted realistic-looking severed limbs, mutilated body parts, and other gruesome props.

Now it was possible to depict all kinds of horror. Faces were shot apart in Martin Scorsese's *Taxi Driver* (1976), and heads rolled in Richard Donner's *The Omen* (1976). Gangster heroes died bloody, violent deaths amid hails of gunfire, detailed gore, and physical carnage in Brian De-Palma's *Scarface* (1983).

The 1980s saw an abundance of "ultraviolence," or extreme graphic violence. In "slasher" horror films, knives, axes, arrows, and chainsaws wreaked bloody havoc in popular thrillers like *Halloween* (1978), *Friday the 13th* (1980), *Nightmare on Elm Street* (1984), and their various sequels and imitators. Ultraviolence overwhelmed

audiences of action/adventure films such as *Predator* (1987), *Lethal Weapon* (1987), *Die Hard* (1988), and their sequels. The 1994 films *Natural Born Killers* and *Pulp Fiction* featured the same graphic, random violence, but it was enacted by murderous social outcasts. The senseless violence of these latter films, and of *Kill Bill* (2003), has been billed as brilliant satire, but their ultra-violent stories have appalled many viewers as well.

Graphically violent films typically receive the R rating, which prevents many younger viewers from seeing them in movie theaters. However, usually within a year of their theatrical release, most of these films reappear on the small screen—on broadcast television or cable networks, or as videocassettes and DVDs. And then they can be, and often are, watched over and over again by people of all ages.

During the late 1970s and 1980s, "slasher" films like Nightmare on Elm Street *became very popular, particularly among young people.*

2

Violence in Music

FOR AMERICAN TEENAGERS, rebelliousness is a fairly common stance. To a greater or lesser degree, asserting one's own sense of independence, in the adolescent years, involves breaking away from parental authority. Many teens conspicuously adopt fashions, hairstyles, and modes of expression that seem designed to shock the sensibilities of the "older generation," and many make a point of criticizing or rejecting the values of their parents.

Popular music has long played an important role in this process, serving as a vehicle by which young people have asserted their independence and rejected the values of their elders symbolically. For some parents and older people, the music of the younger generation presents a real, rather than symbolic, challenge to the social order.

Historically, older generations have railed against supposed decadent and immoral influences in the music their children listened to. It may seem surprising, but musical genres that are today widely respected, such as jazz and rhythm and blues, were once condemned for the immoral messages they supposedly conveyed. Today the focus is on rock and rap, and the major concern is that some songs in these genres encourage and incite young people to violence.

A Brief History

Rock and roll burst onto the musical scene in the 1950s. The new genre combined various influences, including rhythm and blues and country, and it was often criticized for its "jungle beat" and suggestive sexual lyrics. Many conservative groups condemned rock and roll and blamed its irreverent tone for inciting youth to violence and delinquency. On occasion parents and ministers organized album burnings to destroy the offending records.

Most young people, by contrast, welcomed the sounds of the rock revolution and the various musical styles that evolved from it. In the 1960s and beyond, artists like AC/DC, Jimi Hendrix, Deep Purple, and the Who popularized "hard rock," which is characterized by loud guitar playing, distinct melodic phrasing, and pounding percussion. Around the same time "heavy metal" bands, such as Aerosmith, Led Zeppelin, and Black Sabbath, emerged. Their music also emphasized loud, aggressive guitar play and heavy percussion, but with a thickened sound and lyrics that frequently explored dark themes like violence and alienation.

During the 1960s and 1970s many adults became increasingly disturbed by rock lyrics seen as sexually suggestive, drug-related, or inflammatory. Authorities in some cities, including Cleveland, Chicago, Houston, and Atlanta, banned rock concerts altogether in the belief they encouraged drug use or incited rioting. In the 1980s, as song lyrics became

more graphic—particularly in the hard rock and heavy metal genres—parents began to take a closer look at them.

In early 1984 a concerned parent carried a Prince record album into his local Parent-Teacher Association (PTA) meeting in Cincinnati, Ohio. After reading aloud some of the lyrics from the album's inner sleeve, he demanded that the group do something so parents would know whether an album their children wanted to buy featured offensive lyrics. The matter soon made its way to the national organization, and in June the National PTA adopted a resolution urging "recording companies to put a label on record, tape, and cassette covers rating the material contained within with regard to profanity, sex, violence, or vulgarity."[16]

Parents Music Resource Center

The PTA received no response from the music industry. But soon afterward, in May 1985, approximately 20 women, many connected with politics and business in the Washington, D.C., area, formed the Parents Music Resource Center, or PMRC. This advocacy group also believed parents needed information about the controversial content of songs that were entertaining their children. Among the group's spokespersons was Tipper Gore—the wife of Al Gore, then a U.S. senator from Tennessee.

The PMRC wrote to recording industry executives, requesting that the industry establish a ratings system that would let parents identify music with controversial subject matter. The group suggested using letter symbols: V for violence, X for sexually explicit lyrics, O for occult, and D/A for glorification of drug or alcohol use. And the PMRC asked that the system apply to rock concerts as well as all albums. In the letter sent to the various recording companies, the group also rated fifteen songs it considered particularly offensive, referring to them as "The Filthy Fifteen." Two heavy metal songs received the V for violence rating: Mötley Crüe's "Bastard" and Twisted Sister's "We're Not Gonna Take It." Among the other artists targeted for X and D/A ratings were Judas Priest, Prince, Sheena Easton, Madonna, AC/DC, and Black Sabbath.

Senate hearings

The following September, the Senate Committee on Commerce, Science, and Transportation sponsored hearings on rock music lyrics, including suggestions for rating or labeling albums with violent or sexually explicit lyrics. Among those testifying in support of regulating music were members of the PMRC and the National PTA. PMRC member Susan Baker testified about the negative impact of violent lyrics:

> There certainly are many causes for . . . ills in our society, but it is our contention that the pervasive messages aimed at children which promote and glorify suicide, rape, sadomasochism, and so on, have to be numbered among the contributing factors.
>
> Some rock artists actually seem to encourage teen suicide. Ozzie [sic] Osbourne sings "Suicide Solution." Blue Oyster Cult sings "Don't Fear the Reaper." AC/DC sings "Shoot to Thrill." Just last week in Centerpoint, a small Texas town, a young man took his life while listening to the music of AC/DC. He was not the first.[17]

Musicians such as Frank Zappa, Dee Snider (of Twisted Sister), and John Denver testified as well, defending the artist's right to free expression. Zappa noted that he, too, was a parent: "I have got four children. Two of them are here. I want them to grow up in a country where they can think what they want to think, be what they want to be, and not what somebody's wife or somebody in the Government makes them be."[18]

In November 1985 the trade group representing the music industry, the Recording Industry Association of America (RIAA), made an agreement with the National PTA and the Parents Music Resource Center to develop a labeling system. However, almost five years would pass before the music industry issued its official

Frank Zappa was one of many musicians who called the PMRC's record-labeling proposal censorship.

warning label. Meanwhile, many retailers developed their own warning stickers, while others simply removed potentially controversial albums from their shelves.

MTV and music videos

The 1980s also saw the creation of MTV. The cable network—launched on August 1, 1981, by Warner Brothers and American Express—was the first channel devoted exclusively to airing music videos. Though initially targeting rock fans between the ages of fifteen and thirty-five, MTV quickly attracted younger viewers as well. The network's success in capturing and holding the attention of its youthful audience was attributable largely to its "in-your-face" programming: videos that combined frenetic editing techniques (fast cuts, constantly changing angles of view, and special effects) with content that often included controversial music lyrics accompanied by powerful images involving violence or sexuality. Advocacy groups cited concerns about the impact of such programming, particularly on children and teenagers.

Thomas Radecki, founder of the National Coalition on Television Violence (NCTV), was particularly incensed by what he viewed as unhealthy attitudes and behaviors portrayed in many of the music videos. In 1983 he stated, "The message is that violence is normal and okay, that hostile sexual relations between men and women are common and acceptable, that heroes actively engage in torture and murder of others for fun."[19]

The following year, the NCTV issued a report on violence in music videos; it called for federal regulation of rock music on television. According to the study, in 1983 MTV broadcast an average of eighteen acts of violence every hour, and 13 percent of all videos contained violence in which the attacker appeared to take pleasure in committing violence. "The intensive sadistic and sexual violence of a large number of rock music videos is overwhelming," stated Radecki. "It's shocking to see this subculture of hate and violence becoming a fast-growing element of rock music entertainment for the young."[20]

MTV quickly responded to the criticism. In 1984 the network established its own Standards Department to review all MTV content; five years later it adopted a screening system. Videos were rejected for showing illegal drug use, excessive alcohol consumption, or explicit or excessive sex, and for endorsing or promoting violence. Rejected videos could be returned to their producer for reediting. According to Eric Nuzum, in his book *Parental Advisory: Music Censorship in America*, in 1984 one out of every ten videos submitted to MTV was reedited. That number rose to one in three in 1994.

An MTV cameraman records a 1981 concert. The popularity of the channel led to closer examination of the content of music videos.

Parental Advisory labeling

When the RIAA finally unveiled its official Parental Advisory label in 1990, it consisted simply of a black-and-white sticker that read "Explicit Lyrics – Parental Warning." The RIAA recommended that the label be "conspicuously located" on albums containing songs with explicit lyrics, particularly graphic depictions of violence or sex.

However, determination of which albums were to receive a label was left to each of the twenty-nine individual recording companies involved with the agreement. No centralized board like that rating the MPAA's films was in charge. The RIAA defended this system, explaining that the industry had countless numbers of individual songs requiring review each year. The organization maintained that the individual record companies were most familiar with the songs they produced, and most aware of what might be considered offensive in those songs.

Once the official black-and-white Parental Advisory label was in use, the RIAA's worst fears came to pass. Many chain music retailers restricted the sales of "stickered" compact discs (CDs), which by the late 1980s had replaced large vinyl records. Some stores banned anyone under the age of 18 from buying a product bearing the Parental Advisory label. Others refused to sell the albums at all. Among them was the nation's largest retailer, Wal-Mart, which in 1991 announced it would not carry any stickered albums.

Edited music

In order to sell their work, many artists whose albums had received the Parental Advisory label went back to the recording studio and produced the same songs with less offensive lyrics. These edited versions could also be played over the radio airwaves without controversy. And a number of major retail chains that had pulled Parental Advisory–labeled albums from their shelves were willing to sell edited versions.

Some people viewed the edited music albums as censorship, as artists were forced to change what they originally created in order to make it acceptable to retail stores. Others were glad to have the opportunity to buy the "sanitized" songs that their children heard on the radio.

A number of artists complained of internal censorship. Because the Parental Advisory label was seen as a hindrance to sales, recording companies such as Arista, Atlantic, Columbia, Electric, Epic, EMI, MCA, and RCA established review committees to screen new songs for controversial content. Like the Production Code Administration in the first half of the twentieth century, these screening committees were viewed simply as censors.

According to the RIAA website, because a song represents "the artist's personal vision," he or she is left alone in recording songs. However, record companies ask for revisions when "a creative and responsible view of the music demands such a revision. Sometimes songs are simply taken off an album."[21] When both the artist and the record company believe there is "musical and artistic credibility in the whole of the work" but the lyrics are explicit, the RIAA's Parental Advisory label is used.

Lingering concerns

Very few people liked the new system. Advocacy groups complained that the label contained no specific information about album content and no age-appropriate recommendations. The PMRC called on recording industry executives to develop a more detailed ratings system, similar to that used for films and television. The National Institute on Media and the Family pointed out that because the label's use was totally voluntary, an album that did not carry a sticker might still contain objectionable material. Yet another concern was the placement of stickers on the cellophane wrapping of CDs, which allowed for their easy removal.

In 1996 the RIAA and the National Association of Recording Merchandisers (NARM)—a trade organization of music retailers, wholesalers, and distributors—surveyed parents regarding the Parental Advisory label. Based on those results, the RIAA decided to use the advisory label on controversial music videos and to step up its campaign to educate consumers about the label.

Heavy metal misgivings

Meanwhile, concerns about violent music had not abated. During the late 1990s legislators held numerous hearings on topics ranging from violent lyrics to the social impact of music violence to the effectiveness of the Parental Advisory label.

At a hearing in November 1997, Dr. Frank Palumbo represented the American Academy of Pediatrics, which was alarmed about what it viewed as the negative messages and glamorization of harmful lifestyles in teenage music. In his opening remarks Palumbo criticized the state of rock music, noting, "During the past four decades, rock music lyrics have become increasingly explicit—particularly with reference to drugs, sex, violence and even of greater concern, sexual violence."[22]

Palumbo singled out the heavy metal counterculture icon Marilyn Manson in his testimony. He cited some of the shock rocker's lyrics: "'Who said date rape isn't kind,' 'The housewife I will beat' and 'I slit my teenage wrist' are just a sample from two songs,"[23] Palumbo noted. He also discussed his concerns about violent music videos:

> With the advent of MTV and VH-1, not only do we have to listen to violent lyrics that for example degrade women, but we also get to see it acted out in full color. . . . An article in the May 1997 issue of the *Archives of Pediatrics and Adolescent Medicine* documented televised music videos with multiple episodes of violence or weapon carrying. Rock's Guns-N-Roses and Beastie Boys each reached 36 violent episodes in performing just one song.[24]

Singer Marilyn Manson has defended his music as "provocative art" that stimulates debate about the nature of religion and violence.

Marilyn Manson's name was again in the news in 1999, when it was reported that the teenage killers at Columbine High School had been influenced by the shock rocker's music. However, it was another band with vicious song lyrics that gunman Eric Harris mentioned on his website, according to the *Washington Post*: "In oversized lettering, [Harris] quoted from KMFDM, a German rock band whose song 'Waste' includes these lyrics: 'What I don't say I don't do. What I don't do I don't like. What I don't like I waste.' "[25]

The rap on rap

Another musical genre that offended many while also appealing to many began to emerge in the late 1970s. Rap—speaking in rhymes and street slang over a strong rhythmic track—grew out of the black inner-city culture known as hip-hop. It proved extremely popular with white and black youth alike.

Rap's lyrics were rough, often laden with profanity and graphically descriptive of the harshness of life; they frequently addressed themes of poverty, injustice, racism, and police brutality. Songs that drew the sharpest criticism appeared to glorify a culture of gangs, guns, drugs, and violence against women.

As the albums of rap groups such as N.W.A, Public Enemy, and 2 Live Crew gained mainstream popularity during the 1980s and 1990s, conservative groups began to speak out against the controversial lyrics. The PMRC, Focus on the Family, and other like-minded groups called the music pro-drug, pro-gang, and pro-violence. Many critics accused "hard-core rap" and "gangsta rap" of causing inner-city violence, while defenders countered that the violence-laden songs were simply reflecting facts of life for America's urban poor.

One particularly controversial song was performed by former N.W.A member Ice-T. Released in 1992, "Cop Killer" contained lyrics that appeared to encourage and glorify the murder of police officers. Several groups and police organizations protested, calling for a boycott of all products made by Time Warner, whose recording company produced the album. Although the Ice-T album was eventually recalled and reissued without the offending track, the performer did not apologize for the lyrics.

The tell-it-like-it-is hip-hop culture has produced other controversial performers, including Limp Bizkit, Dr. Dre, and Eminem—all of whom have been criticized for violent lyrics promoting hatred and violence against women. Eminem's song "Kim," for example, contains a graphic (though fictional) description of the artist murdering his estranged wife.

Yet rap has gone "mainstream," replacing pop in 2001 as the third most popular music genre—the same year Eminem won three Grammy awards. In 2002 he performed the song "Without Me" at the awards program, although the profanities had to be bleeped out of the television broadcast.

Rap singer Ice-T agreed to pull the controversial song "Cop Killer" from his 1992 album Body Count, *but he distributed copies of the song for free at his concerts.*

A pervasive message of violence?

Even with controversial music genres like heavy metal and rap, RIAA head Hilary Rosen insists that very few albums actually receive the Parental Advisory label. In testimony before the Committee on Governmental Affairs of the United States Senate, she noted, "[D]espite the emphasis at these hearings on recordings with explicit content, they comprise a relatively small portion of our industry's output. In an average retail store, only 500 of 110,000 titles—less than one-half of one percent—carry the Parental Advisory Label."[26]

But even if the content is not graphic or explicit enough to receive the Parental Advisory label, shock rock and rap can be harmful, says the American Academy of Child and Adolescent Psychiatry (AACAP). Their messages of hate and violence, particularly against women, and presentation of suicide as a "solution" can affect teenagers who already feel alienated or depressed, the AACAP maintains.

The shock value of violence continues to sell music videos for MTV, despite its screening programs. In a 1997 analysis of MTV music by R.H. DuRant and colleagues, nearly one-fourth of the videos showed overt violence, with "attractive role models being aggressors in more than 80 percent of the violent videos."[27] Today MTV is the most watched television network throughout the world, reaching more than 350 million households in 140 countries. And, critics charge, it is broadcasting a message of violence.

3

Violence in Interactive Media

RAPID ADVANCES IN microchip technology have led to the development of a popular form of entertainment that would have been difficult to imagine only a few decades ago: realistic, interactive games that are played out on computer and TV screens. Today fans of these games can test their skill and their nerve in a variety of settings, from the football field to the battlefield. As with violence in movies, television shows, and popular songs, violence in interactive media is a source of increasing concern for researchers, social critics, and advocates for children.

Interactive media refers to computer and other electronic systems in which a person manipulates electronic images on a screen using a joystick, controller, or keyboard. His or her actions and responses determine what happens next on the screen. People use interactive media whenever they play computer or video games or surf websites on the Internet.

Video and computer games

Video games include games played in arcades; on handheld, portable systems such as Game Boy; and on separate machines, or "game platforms," that are hooked up to a television. By the first years of the 21st century, game platforms included Sony PlayStation and PlayStation 2, Sega Dreamcast, Nintendo GameCube, and Microsoft Xbox. The Xbox game system has its own hard drive and allows access to the Internet.

A single video game platform usually accommodates up to four players; some can be networked together so that even more people can play. Computer games can be played alone or with others on a network or over the Internet. Today many of the same games are available for play on computers and video game platforms, but when the industry was just beginning, video and computer games were different from one another.

Today's multibillion-dollar video game industry dates to 1972, when an electrical engineer named Nolan Bushness founded a company called Atari. Within the year Bushness had a best-selling product on his hands. Called Pong, this very first video game bore only a passing resemblance to table tennis: Using dials, players moved two short lines (the paddles) to bounce a small square (the ball) across the television screen.

Soon other companies had jumped into the business, and an assortment of increasingly sophisticated action/adventure, driving, fighting, puzzle, role-playing, sports, and strategy games were produced for an eager market. By the end of the 1980s interactive video games had become one of the most popular forms of entertainment among teens.

Concerns about simulated mayhem

Some video games popular during the early 1980s—such as the action/adventure offering Super Mario Brothers and the fighting game Zelda 64—featured characters that "died" and came back to life, an element of unreality that certain observers found disturbing. But no one could deny the broad appeal of video game play.

In the early 1990s, critics began to raise concerns about the violence in fighting games. They pointed to video games such as Mortal Kombat (1993), which required players to "finish" their opponents by dismembering them, and Night Trap (1994), which featured violence against women. At Senate hearings on video game violence, legislators watched clips of these games and debated whether to create laws that would help consumers become better informed of their violent content.

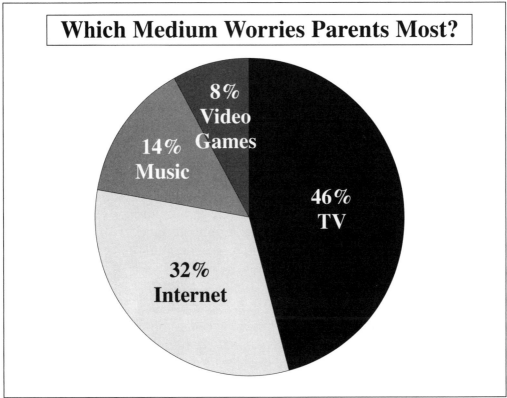

Which Medium Worries Parents Most?

8% Video Games

14% Music

46% TV

32% Internet

Source: Annenberg Public Policy Center of the University of Pennsylvania, Media in the Home 2000: The Fifth Annual Survey of Parents and Children.

Fighting games were also being created for computers, which were becoming more sophisticated by the late 1980s. With the introduction of the CD-ROM, software designers found they could create games with realistic three-dimensional settings, along with improved sound and graphics.

In 1992 the software team of John Romero and John Carmack, who had founded their own game company, id Software, released Wolfenstein 3-D, a "first-person shooter" computer game. In a first-person shooter game, the player controls the game and experiences the action through the eyes of the main character—whose mission is to kill or be killed. The character in Wolfenstein 3-D is a marine tasked with tracking down and shooting Nazis in a dungeon.

The game developers, however, were not satisfied with Wolfenstein. Romero told Paul Keegan of the *New York*

Times, "[W]hen we started playing, it was like, 'We have to have more blood, more violence in there.' It seemed real, but we needed to show the guys dying."[28]

Their next first-person shooter game did just that. Released in 1993, Doom was the first three-dimensional game that could be played over a computer network, and id Software marketed it by providing its first stages, or "levels," as a free download. Intentional "cracks" in the source code allowed gamers to hack into the program to create their own levels. The company followed up with another popular first-person shooter game, Quake, in 1996. All recorded brisk sales. By 1999 a total of 2.7 million copies of Doom and its sequel Doom II had been sold in the United States—and these numbers did not include the free download copies.

ESRB ratings

As computer and video games incorporated more realistic violence, public criticism of them grew louder. After the Senate held hearings on video game violence, several game

Video games like this one, in which the action is seen from the player's perspective, are known as "first-person shooters."

manufacturers set out to develop a ratings system that would address concerns and forestall federal legislation imposing restrictions. In March 1994 several industry representatives met with Senators Joseph Lieberman and Herbert Kohl and presented them with a proposed ratings system.

Soon afterward the Entertainment Software Rating Board (ESRB) was established by the major trade organization for the video game industry—the Interactive Digital Software Association, or IDSA. (The trade group would be renamed the Entertainment Software Association, or ESA, in 2003.) The IDSA also created an Advertising Code of Conduct that required ESRB rating information to be placed on packaging and in advertising.

Although the video game ratings system has undergone some changes since it was first instituted in 1994, it currently consists of five ESRB rating symbols and more than 30 content descriptors. The descriptors—short phrases that appear on the back of the game's package—give detailed information on potentially offensive game content, such as "animated blood," "comic mischief," or "strong language."

The rating symbols are based on age. EC stands for Early Childhood, indicating the game is intended for young children. The E rating refers to Everyone. (In January 1998 it replaced KA, or Kids to Adults.) E-rated games, considered appropriate for ages six years and up, may contain minimal violence, slapstick comedy, and some crude language.

Games that contain some violence, profanity, and "mild sexual themes" receive the T, or Teen rating. T-rated games are considered appropriate for ages thirteen and up.

The M, or Mature-rating symbol, refers to games geared for ages seventeen and up. These games contain intense violence, profanity, and mature sexual themes. Games considered inappropriate for persons under eighteen receive the AO, or Adults Only rating. AO games contain graphic violence and sexual themes.

If a game has been released without a rating but will be receiving one later, the RP rating is applied. The symbol designates Rating Pending.

To obtain a rating, the game's publisher fills out a detailed questionnaire about the product's content and sends it and a segment of actual footage to the ESRB for review. Three trained people who have no ties to the video game industry view the segment independently. Each determines the appropriate rating symbol, taking into consideration content categories such as violence, sex, language, and substance abuse. At least two raters must apply the same rating for it to be considered an appropriate category. They also determine whether content descriptors are needed.

Senators Joseph Lieberman and Herbert Kohl, here watching a video game, supported ratings for video games played on home game platforms.

Murder simulators

The M rating is usually applied to graphic first-person shooter games, which Lt. Col. Dave Grossman refers to as "murder simulators." Grossman, who has taught courses to the military on the psychology of killing, believes first-person shooter games should not be in the hands of young children. The games teach them how to shoot like soldiers, he says, moving quickly from one target to another, with an emphasis on head shots.

Grossman claimed there was a direct link between violent video games and the shooting ability of Michael Carneal, perpetrator of the 1998 school shooting in West

Paducah, Kentucky. In his 1999 book *Stop Teaching Our Kids to Kill*, Grossman states:

> Fourteen-year-old Michael Carneal steals a gun from a neighbor's house, brings it to school, and fires eight shots into a student prayer meeting that is breaking up. Prior to stealing the gun, he had never shot a real handgun in his life. The FBI says that the average experienced law enforcement officer, in the average shootout, at an average range of seven yards, hits with approximately one bullet in five. So how many hits did Michael Carneal make? He fired eight shots; he got eight hits, on eight different kids. Five of them were head shots, and the other three were upper torso. The result was three dead and one paralyzed for life. I tell law enforcement officers about this when I train them, and they are stunned....
>
> How did Michael Carneal acquire this kind of killing ability? Simple: practice. At the tender age of fourteen he had practiced killing literally thousands of people. His simulators were point-and-shoot video games he played for hundreds of hours in video arcades and in the comfort of his own home.[29]

Pediatrician Michael Rich, head of the Center on Media and Child Health at Harvard University, agrees that the interactive capability of violent video and computer games allows players to practice killing. "With video games, you're not only passively receiving attitudes and behaviors, you're rehearsing them,"[30] he says.

Concerns over the possible connection between video game violence and real-life violence increased after the Columbine High School tragedy. The Columbine High School shooters were avid players of the Doom and Quake games, the press reported. The website of one of the shooters contained add-on levels for Doom and Quake, along with instructions for users, such as "The platoon guarding the teleporter out is VERY large, so beware. Good luck marine, and don't forget, KILL 'EM AAAAALLLL!!!!!"[31]

Dedicated gamers quickly responded to the charges. "Everyone is always quick to point out murderers that play violent video games, but no one ever thinks of the millions of people that play video games and aren't murderers,"[32] said a gamer quoted in a story by Janelle Brown for Salon.com.

Software developer Greg Costikyan argues that playing violent games allows players to act out violent impulses, "to hunt and shoot and kill—in a way that harms no one."[33] People playing these games know it is fantasy, he says. They are "blowing up pixels. They're killing bitmaps. They're shooting at software subroutines."[34]

When a *Harper's* magazine essay attacked video games for contributing to school violence, New Jersey teen Joe Stavitsky responded in a letter to the editor:

> As a geek, I can tell you that none of us play video games to learn how (or why) to shoot people. For us, video games do not cause violence; they prevent it. We see games as a perfectly safe release from a physically violent reaction to the daily abuse leveled at us.[35]

Increasing the shock value

In 2001 and 2002 the top-selling games were also the most violent. They featured death, murder, and mayhem and rewarded players for vicious behaviors. A description of the worst offenders appeared on the Media Awareness Network website:

> [P]layers in Grand Theft Auto 3 (the best-selling game ever for PlayStation 2) earn points by carjacking, and stealing drugs from street people and pushers. In Carmageddon, players are rewarded for mowing down pedestrians—sounds of cracking bones add to the realistic effect. . . . In the game Postal, players act out the part of the Postal Dude, who earns points by randomly shooting everyone who appears—including people walking out of church, and members of a high school band. Postal Dude is programmed to say, "Only my gun understands me."[36]

State representative Mary Lou Dickerson of Washington finds these games and others like it offensive. "A lot of these games are just plain sick," she told Lee Hochberg of Oregon Public Broadcasting. "They're sick, they're violent, they're racist, and they really have no business in the hands of a 12-year-old."[37]

Joseph Lieberman, a U.S. senator from Connecticut, agrees. "The content of many cutting edge games is becoming more and more vivid, violent, and offensive to our most basic values," he said in 2002 at a Capitol Hill news conference. "This relatively small but highly popular minority is not just pushing the envelope—they are shooting, torturing and napalming it beyond all recognition, and beyond all decency."[38]

Some national retailers, such as Sears, have banned the sale of M-rated games at their stores. The retail giant Wal-Mart, which sells about 25 percent of computer and video games bought in the United States, is big enough to exert some control over the content of the products on its shelves. The company's purchasing managers review video and computer games before their release, and Wal-Mart refuses to carry any products that fail to meet its guidelines. In some cases game companies have toned down more sexually explicit games in order to ensure that the large retailer will carry them.

Pervasive influences

In 2002, according to the ESRB website, 63 percent of all rated games received an E for Everyone rating, 27 percent received a T for Teen rating, 8 percent received an M for Mature rating, and 2 percent received an EC for Early Childhood rating. Sixteen of the top twenty best-selling games in 2002 were rated for everyone or for teens.

But some researchers believe the ratings do not reflect the amount of violent content in games. A study by Craig A. Anderson and colleagues in 2001 reported that 60 to 90 percent of video games have violent themes, although the type of violence varies.

Meanwhile, studies show that video game playing is very much a part of American life. About 67 percent of households with children own a video game system, and 60 percent of Americans over the age of six play games on the computer. More than 221 million computer and video games—or almost two games for every home—were sold in 2002.

Video and computer games have had a great impact on children and families, says David Walsh, founder of the National Institute on Media and the Family (NIMF). Since 1996 the organization has worked to provide research, information, and education on the media to families. A survey taken in 2002 revealed that video game play is a large part of Americans' lives: 87 percent of children in grades four through twelve played video games, with 96 percent of boys and 78 percent of girls playing regularly.

Failing grades

Among NIMF's projects is a yearly review of video and computer games, titled the "MediaWise Video Game Report Card." The report card grades the video game industry in several areas: accuracy of ratings, effectiveness in educating parents about game content, and effectiveness of retailers in restricting access by children to Mature-rated games.

In December 2002, NIMF gave the industry an F. "This year's grade reflects the dramatic increase in violent games and, in particular, games rewarding violence against women,"[39] the report's authors said. Grand Theft Auto games were singled out, particularly Vice City, "in which gratuitous violence toward women and police is rewarded and discrimination against the Haitian community is encouraged."[40]

The 2003 MediaWise Video Game Report Card also criticized the industry for not assigning the AO rating to games like Grand Theft Auto: Vice City and the recently released Manhunt. Although both are brutally violent games, they received the M rating instead. (Most major retailers will not sell AO games.)

Internet issues

Many parents worry about the wide range of information their children may be exposed to on the internet.

The Internet offers a wide range of media—games, music, television shows, and film. Game websites allow strangers and friends to play video games online; games can also be downloaded for individual use. File-sharing sites al-

low the downloading of digital song files or of film clips. On the Internet, ratings and retailer policies cannot be easily enforced, and the possibility exists for even very young children to obtain controversial and even harmful materials.

Among American adults, the greatest concern about the Internet is that it can allow dangerous strangers to make contact with children, according to a 2000 poll by National Public Radio, the Kaiser Family Foundation, and Harvard's Kennedy School of Government. More than half of the people polled also agreed with the statement "the federal government needs to regulate what is on the Internet more than television and newspapers because the Internet can be used to gain easier access to dangerous information."[41] The dangerous information cited included pornography, information on how to build bombs, and hate speech.

The same poll showed that only 39 percent of kids were concerned about violent video games, compared with 56 percent of adults. More than half of the kids said they spent less time outdoors because of computers and knew kids who were addicted to video or computer games. Almost a third of those aged ten to seventeen admitted having seen a pornographic website on the Internet, even if by accident.

In September 2003, America Online sponsored a poll of kids aged seven to twelve that evaluated their Internet use. Nearly half (46 percent) reported that they went online four days a week, and 20 percent went online every day. A large majority (87 percent) used the Internet to play games online, and those numbers are expected to grow. Clearly, any effective effort to limit children's access to violent interactive media must take into account not just video games sold in stores, but also the much more difficult to monitor online world.

4

Linking Media Violence with Real-Life Violence

IS THERE A causal connection between violence depicted in the entertainment media and real-life violence? Does watching numerous acts of on-screen violence cause children to behave more aggressively or hold more antisocial attitudes and values? Since the 1950s, researchers have sought to answer questions such as these.

"The debate is over," the American Psychiatric Association declared in 2003. "Over the last three decades, the one overriding finding in research on the mass media is that exposure to media portrayals of violence increases aggressive behavior in children."[42]

But not everyone agrees with that assessment. Some critics have found fault with the studies that purport to show a definitive connection between media violence and real-life violence. And even among those who concede that such a connection does exist, there is wide disagreement on how important a role media violence plays in contributing to aggressive or violent behavior.

In 1993 the American Psychological Association (APA) released a report describing specific negative effects that it said media violence can have on youth. The report stated that young people who view long hours of violent programming are susceptible to behavior changes such as desensitization, fearfulness, and increased aggression.

Desensitization

Some researchers believe that when young people view media violence over and over again, they can become emotionally numb—or desensitized—to its impact. As the young people become used to seeing depictions of fights, killings, and deaths, these researchers say, they become increasingly callous, unable to feel sympathy for the victim or understand the victim's fear, pain, or loss. Over the long term, they may become indifferent to violent behavior and come to believe that violence is an acceptable solution in stressful or frustrating situations.

In his book *Stop Teaching Our Kids to Kill*, Dave Grossman asserts that playing violent video games for hours on end also desensitizes children. "Images of violence as "cool" . . . result in less empathy, compassion, and understanding for human suffering,"[43] he writes. Such desensitization may lead to what researchers call "the bystander effect," in which someone who watches a great deal of media violence is more likely to turn his or her back on someone in need.

Writer Gerard Jones is among the critics who are skeptical of the idea that fictional violence desensitizes children to actual violence. "Children know real pain and real loss

when they see them. Young people who've grown up witnessing thousands of acts of imaginary violence show no impairment to their emotional or cognitive reactions when real violence enters their lives," Jones claims. "Studies that have endeavored to back up the desensitization idea show only that exposure to filmed violence can desensitize children to more filmed violence. . . . But none of those studies show any correspondence between desensitization to mediated violence and desensitization to personal reality."[44]

Fearfulness

A 1990 study by George Gerbner and Nancy Signorielli found that children who watched five or more hours of television daily were more fearful of the world around them than were those who watched three hours or less. The study also showed that about twenty violent acts occurred per hour on the shows the children were watching. This meant heavy viewers were being subjected to a great deal of violence.

Images of violence on news broadcasts and in entertainment—even if the exposure is relatively brief—can, under certain circumstances, traumatize young children, says Dr. Joanne Cantor, an expert on the effects of mass media upon youth. Such emotional trauma can cause sleep disturbances, nightmares, anxiety, and depression.

Repeated exposure to media violence may result in what George Gerbner and his colleagues have referred to as "mean world syndrome," by which people come to see the world as a much more dangerous place than it really is, and come to believe that other people cannot be trusted. For example, while statistically the chances of becoming a murder victim in the United States are quite small, the abundance of fictional murders depicted on television may create the impression that the danger is great. Similarly, other violent crimes are overrepresented in the media. Thus, some researchers claim, heavy viewers of TV may be overly fearful of becoming victims of crime.

Again, however, other researchers are not so certain that intense television viewing *causes* fearfulness. They point out that some of the heaviest viewers of television come

from the ranks of the poor, uneducated, and unemployed—and that these people tend to live in high-crime neighborhoods. Thus, critics of the mean world hypothesis argue, the fear of these people has less to do with intense television viewing than with real conditions where they live—and frequently from their personal experiences with crime.

The number of murders depicted in movies and on television may lead people to conclude that the world is more dangerous than it really is. Shown here is a scene from the film Taxi Driver.

Aggression and violent television

A great deal of research has focused on proving that watching violent television programming causes aggressive behavior. One of the best-known studies was published in the early 1960s by Albert Bandura and colleagues. The researchers showed a group of nursery-school-age children a film of a young woman punching, kicking, and yelling at a five-foot inflatable punching doll called Bobo. Later, when the children were placed in a room containing a Bobo doll and other toys, they imitated the aggressive behavior—hitting, kicking, and yelling at the doll. In contrast, a control group that had not seen the film played quietly in the room with other toys, ignoring the doll. Bandura concluded that observing aggressive behavior can cause young children to imitate it.

Critics contend that the Bobo doll experiment says nothing about the possible effects of TV violence on children in the real world. First of all, the critics argue, young children are likely to become very excited and to act out when they see anything new. In addition, they say, there is no proof that displays of aggression directed at an inflatable doll would translate to actual aggression or violence against a real person. Indeed, toys such as the Bobo doll are designed to be punched and kicked and to bounce back up after being knocked down.

In general, those who are skeptical of media violence experiments question whether results obtained in laboratory settings have much predictive value in real-world situations. For example, studies have shown that exposure to violent images increases heart rate, speeds up respiration, and raises blood pressure. While these are physiological reactions that

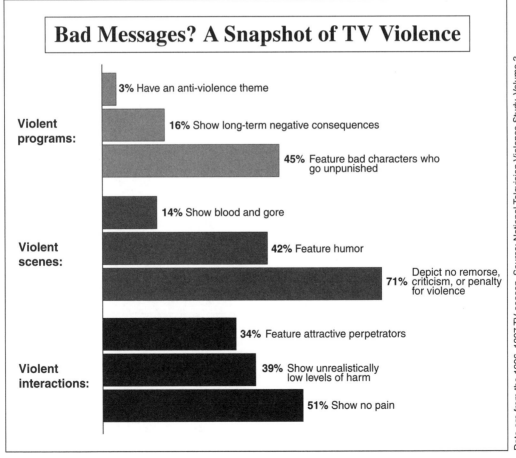

Bad Messages? A Snapshot of TV Violence

Violent programs:
- **3%** Have an anti-violence theme
- **16%** Show long-term negative consequences
- **45%** Feature bad characters who go unpunished

Violent scenes:
- **14%** Show blood and gore
- **42%** Feature humor
- **71%** Depict no remorse, criticism, or penalty for violence

Violent interactions:
- **34%** Feature attractive perpetrators
- **39%** Show unrealistically low levels of harm
- **51%** Show no pain

Data are from the 1996–1997 TV season. Source: National Television Violence Study, Volume 3.

would take place right before a real-life fight, critics wonder whether they are really a valid measure of study participants' short-term aggressiveness, much less whether exposure to such images affects long-term patterns of aggression. Journalist Richard Rhodes finds another reason for regarding most of the media violence studies as inconsistent and fundamentally flawed. Their results, Rhodes claims, "don't account for the powerful effect called 'researcher expectation,' whereby the subject easily guesses what the researcher wants him to do and behaves that way."[45]

Jib Fowles, a professor of communication at the University of Houston at Clear Lake, examined the media violence literature for his 1999 book *The Case for Television Violence*. Fowles found that, despite widespread claims that as many as twenty-five hundred studies have linked media violence with aggressive behavior, there are actually no more than two hundred such studies. In addition, Fowles concluded, few of those are "real-world" studies as opposed to laboratory experiments, and fewer still followed subjects over an extended period of time.

One widely cited real-world study that did follow subjects over a long period of time was conducted by University of Michigan psychologists Leonard Eron and L. Rowell Huesmann. In 1960 Eron surveyed the viewing habits of more than eight hundred eight-year-old in upstate New York. He found that the boys who watched violent television programming tended to be more aggressive on the playground and in the classroom (no correlation was found for girls). Eron was joined by Huesmann in follow-up studies made in 1971 and again in 1982. The researchers reported that the aggressive eight-year-old boys had become even more aggressive as nineteen-year-olds (as rated by peers), and as thirty-year-olds (as determined by their involvement in incidents of domestic violence, child abuse, and criminal arrests).

Eron and Huesmann maintained that there is a clear association between watching violent television and aggressive behavior. "When violent action is all [children] see," noted

Eron, "the lesson they learn is that everybody does it and this is the way to behave."[46]

Huesmann also believes that exposure to media violence during childhood can negatively affect viewers years later as adults. He reported on the results of a study of children ages six to ten made in 1977 and 1978, and of the same individuals as adults in the early 1990s. Those exposed to a great deal of TV violence as children, Huesmann found, were more likely to display aggressive and antisocial behavior later in life. Men who, as children, had been heavy watchers of violent television were convicted of crimes three times more often than other men. Women who had watched a great deal of TV violence were four times more likely to have punched, beaten, or choked another adult. "[E]very violent TV show," researchers concluded, "increases a little-bit the likelihood of a child growing up to behave more aggressively."[47]

Researcher Jeffrey Johnson of Columbia University reported similar findings in a long-term study tracking a large group from adolescence into adulthood. Johnson reported, "We found that teenagers who, at mean age 14, watched more than three hours a day of television were much more likely than those who watched less than one hour a day of television to commit subsequent acts of aggression against other people."[48]

As has been the case with other television-violence studies, however, some experts do not accept as valid the results obtained by Eron and Huesmann and by Johnson. For example, psychologist and media researcher Guy Cumberbatch, director of the Communications Research Group, based in Birmingham, England, argued that the number of teens in Johnson's study who watched less than an hour of television per day was too small to draw valid conclusions. Similarly, Jib Fowles of the University of Houston notes that in their study of third graders in upstate New York, Eron and Huesmann emphasized a correlation between boys' viewing of violent television at age eight and their aggressiveness at age nineteen in only one of three measurements that the researchers used (the other two measures revealed no correlation), and no correlation was found among girls—which, Fowles claims, adds up to weak evidence for a link. Additionally, many skeptics say that the links studies have found between watching a great deal of violent television (or other violent media, for that matter) and actual violent behavior may not reflect cause and effect. Instead, these skeptics say, individuals who are aggressive or violent for other reasons may simply prefer violent entertainment.

Aggression and violent music and video games

Far more media-effects research has centered on television than on popular music or video games. Nevertheless, some studies have suggested that young people who listen to a great deal of music with violent lyrics or spend a lot of time playing violent video games may be more aggressive or hostile than their peers who do not.

Psychology professor Craig A. Anderson and colleagues reported, in the *Journal of Personality and Social Psychology*, that listening to violent song lyrics may cause feelings of aggression and hostility. The study assessed participants'

The music of rap star Eminem has been criticized as promoting violence against women, homosexuals, and others.

responses to violent lyrics in songs by such bands as Tool, Suicidal Tendencies, the Beastie Boys, and Run-D.M.C. It measured effects through various psychological tests, such as how participants completed a word fragment (for example, did they associate "h-t" with the more aggressive "hit," or with the neutral "hat"?). As with other media violence experiments, however, precisely how the results might correlate with actual violent or aggressive behavior remains difficult to say, critics maintain. Some psychologists claim that songs with violent lyrics, like other violent media, have a cathartic effect—that is, they provide a

Experts disagree about whether the slapstick of Three Stooges movies should be considered harmless entertainment or disturbing violence.

release for anger and negative feelings—an idea Anderson and his colleagues reject.

Experts generally agree that the potential impact of violent video games on youth is greater than the possible impact of violent lyrics—and may even be greater than the impact of violent movies or television. This is because video games require active participation rather than passive observation.

In the *Journal of Personality and Social Psychology*, Craig A. Anderson and Karen Dill reported that college students who spent a lot of time playing violent video games were more aggressive in their general behavior than were those who did not play as much. The researchers also set up an experiment to compare the behavior of college students after playing either a violent video game (Wolfenstein 3D) or a nonviolent game (Myst). After playing the game, each student participated in a "competitive reaction time task" with another student. The winner was told he or she could blast the loser with a noise, which could be as loud and last as long as the winner wanted. Anderson and Dill reported that students who played the violent video game blasted their opponents longer and louder than did those who had played the nonviolent game. These laboratory results led the researchers to conclude "that exposure to violent video games can increase aggressive behavior."[49]

Again, though, critics wonder whether a proxy for real aggression—in this case, blasting peers with a loud noise—has much relevance to the question of possible real-world effects. And, in interpreting the results of their questionnaire on college students' violent video game playing, Anderson and Dill claimed, for example, that the Mario Brothers game "involves violence in the sense that the player typically spends a considerable amount of time destroying other creatures."[50] Many video game aficionados would consider that interpretation ridiculous and would describe the game simply as one in which the main character jumps on turtles and bumps his head on blocks to get points. (Critics have frequently leveled the charge that the cumulative results of various media violence studies are weakened by the lack of standardization in the way social scientists define violence. Some, for example, count Three Stooges slapstick routines or Road Runner cartoons as violence, whereas others do not.)

Beyond a reasonable doubt?

It is probable that there will always be credible observers like science writer Richard Rhodes, who insists that "no direct, causal link between exposure to mock violence in the media and subsequent violent behavior has ever been demonstrated,"[51] or Professor Jonathan Freedman of the University of Toronto, who believes that the "bulk of the research does not show that television or movie violence has any negative effects."[52] Part of the reason for this is the inherent difficulty in establishing, with absolute certainty, a cause-and-effect relationship between events that take place over a long period of time, particularly when many variables are involved. In addition, as Rowell Huesmann and Leonard Eron explain, "[Social] science never produces uniform results. There are always some number of studies that show no effect."[53]

That said, the majority of social scientists who have weighed in on the issue publicly believe that there is a causal connection between young people's consumption of violent media and increased aggressiveness—in *some* children. And a variety of groups representing medical and mental health professionals have added their voices to the chorus. In July 2000, at a Public Health Summit held in Washington, D.C., representatives of the American Medical Association, American Academy of Pediatrics, American Psychological Association, American Psychiatric Association, American Academy of Family Physicians, and American Academy of Child & Adolescent Psychiatry released a joint statement that said, in part:

> At this time, well over 1000 studies—including reports from the Surgeon General's office, the National Institute of Mental Health, and numerous studies conducted by leading figures within our medical and public health organizations—our own members—point overwhelmingly to a causal connection between media violence and aggressive behavior in some children. The conclusion of the public health community, based on over 30 years of research, is that viewing entertainment violence can lead to increases in aggressive attitudes, values and behavior, particularly in children.[54]

It should be noted that the number of valid studies on media violence effects is a matter of dispute. In his 2002 book *Media Violence and Its Effect on Aggression: Assessing the Scientific Evidence*, for example, Jonathan Freedman writes, "There aren't over a thousand studies. There are about 200 studies, give or take a few."[55]

Copycat crimes

One point that is beyond dispute is that in a small number of cases, individuals have imitated an act of violence they saw in a movie or on television. For example, in 1993, in a widely publicized case in England, two eleven-year-old boys abducted and killed a two-year-old toddler, apparently after viewing a videotape of *Child's Play 3*. That movie tells the story of a pair of boys who fight and kill an evil doll. In 1995 a New York City subway clerk died after teens set him on fire, an act that had been depicted in the recently released movie *Money Train*. That same year, after viewing the TV movie *Helter Skelter*, four youths went on a killing spree that claimed four lives. Interestingly, Charles Manson, the mastermind of the 1969 murders upon which *Helter Skelter* was based, claimed to have received communications and instructions from a Beatles record. In 1998 a suicide note left by a twelve-year-old in Maryland cited the character Kenny, who dies a violent death each week in the cartoon comedy *South Park*; another eleven-year-old who hanged himself the same year and who was apparently also inspired by the Kenny character reportedly remarked a few days before his death that it was all right if he died because he would be back the following week. Within three years of the release of Oliver Stone's ultraviolent 1994 film *Natural Born Killers*, fifteen murders—in locations ranging from Nebraska to Paris—were attributed to young people who claimed they had been imitating the film's characters. Several fatal school shootings, including those at Columbine and West Paducah, have also been blamed on violent video

Chucky, a mechanical doll possessed by a demon, sneaks up on a victim in the 1991 movie Child's Play 3. *In 1993, a pair of eleven-year-old boys acted out a scene from the film by murdering a two-year-old.*

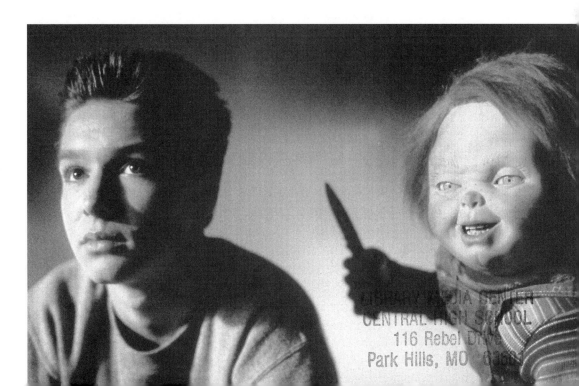

games such as Doom and Quake, and violent movies such as *The Matrix* and *The Basketball Diaries*.

In some of these incidents, it is impossible to deny a link between the fictionalized act of violence and the real-life act. At the same time, however, it would be a mistake to draw sweeping conclusions about the media's role in increasing violent behavior based solely on the evidence of copycat crimes. In some instances, the perpetrators of copycat crimes are children who apparently do not understand the consequences of their acts—who do not know, for example, that if they hang themselves they will not come back the following week, like a cartoon character. Others who have committed copycat crimes were clearly emotionally troubled, even mentally ill, before they saw a particular movie or TV show or played a certain video game. While it can be said with a degree of certainty that, in the absence of the media depiction, they would not have committed the crime or act of violence in the particular manner they did, it cannot be said for certain that they would not have committed a similar act of violence in a different manner.

As Henry Jenkins, director of Comparative Media Studies at the Massachusetts Institute of Technology, explained in reference to Eric Harris and Dylan Klebold:

> Media images may have given [the Columbine shooters] symbols to express their rage and frustration, but the media did not create the rage or generate their alienation. What sparked the violence was not something they saw on the internet or on television, not some song lyric or some sequence from a movie, but things that really happened to them. [56]

Journalist Richard Rhodes holds similar views. People do not learn violence from the media, Rhodes insists, but from "personal violent encounters, beginning with the brutalization of children by their parents or peers."[57]

"When somebody commits a violent crime, you can't point to just one cause," says Joanne Cantor, a media violence researcher and communications professor at the University of Wisconsin. But, she adds, "I think these things can have really devastating effects on really vulnerable

A soldier lies dead in this scene from a video game. Supporters of video games argue that, rather than causing violent behavior, the games provide an appropriate outlet for aggression.

people. . . . If people are saying they were influenced by that movie, that movie was probably on their mind when they were planning these things."[58]

Nevertheless, the possibility that a small number of troubled people might imitate fictional violence will probably never dissuade filmmakers, producers, recording artists, or authors from turning out violent entertainment—particularly when millions of others consume the same products and are seemingly unaffected (and, as certain writers claim, fictional violence may even help some youths work through their troubles without enacting real violence). The Free Expression Policy Project website notes, "It is impossible to predict which episodes or descriptions will be imitated by unstable individuals, and equally impossible to ban every book, movie, magazine article, song, game, or other cultural product that somebody might imitate."[59]

Youth violence: many causes

Even among those experts who believe that a causal connection between media violence and increased aggression is firmly established, no one claims that fictional depictions of violence are the primary cause of real-life violence. In fact, many believe that violence in the media is not even a significant contributor to youth violence. That essentially was the conclusion of *Youth Violence: A Report of the Surgeon General*, released in 2001 by Dr. David Satcher. The study had been requested shortly after the Columbine killings, and many people believed it would find media violence to blame for the school shootings. Instead it downplayed media violence as a potential factor in causing youth violence. "For some people [media violence] was in their minds the major purpose of this report," Satcher noted. "We did not find the media to be a major factor—(just) a factor."[60]

The report concluded that factors most likely to cause aggression and violence in children are "substance abuse, being male, physical aggression, low family socioeconomic status or poverty and antisocial parents." For teenagers the "strongest risk factors are weak ties to conventional peers, ties to antisocial or delinquent peers, belonging to a gang, and involvement in other criminal acts."[61] In an indication of the relative importance the surgeon general attributed to the media as a cause of violence, the report relegated the topic to an appendix, rather than dedicating a chapter to the subject. This treatment irritated many critics of the entertainment industry, and calls for regulating violent media content have continued unabated.

5

Regulating the Media

OVER THE PAST half century, public concerns about the potentially harmful effects of violent media, particularly on children, have inspired debates among local, state, and federal lawmakers. Many legislators have proposed bills affecting various aspects of the media, but few such bills have passed. Most U.S. lawmakers are reluctant to regulate the media because they believe such an action would violate the First Amendment to the U.S. Constitution.

First Amendment issues

Among other rights, the First Amendment guarantees freedom of speech, and that guarantee applies not just to individuals and the press. The courts have consistently said that the First Amendment protects any medium that communicates an idea or message, including television, motion pictures, and music.

For many years the First Amendment has protected the entertainment industry from government censorship. Most people feel strongly that the government should not regulate the industry at all. "It is anathema to the First Amendment," said Supreme Court justice William O. Douglas, "to allow government any role of censorship over newspapers, magazines, books, art, music, TV, radio or any other aspect of the press."[62]

Others say it is appropriate for the government to place some limits on free expression, especially when the result

Groups like the American Civil Liberties Union argue that government efforts to regulate violent content in the media violate the First Amendment.

or product is offensive. But these people hold the minority viewpoint. According to a survey by the First Amendment Center, about 60 percent of respondents said they support First Amendment freedoms, while only 34 percent said the First Amendment sometimes goes too far.

Exceptions to the rule

While the First Amendment's guarantees of free speech are far reaching, regulation of speech has been allowed under certain narrow circumstances—for example, when the speech consists of so-called fighting words, causes lawless activity, defames someone, or is considered obscene. Legislation whose goal is to protect the welfare of children has also passed court review in some cases. For example, the courts have upheld the right of states to prohibit the sale of obscene and pornographic material to young people.

Some legislators have attempted to regulate violent media content by defining it as obscene. Media products that contain violence, they argue, need to be restricted to protect children from harmful effects.

However, groups like the American Civil Liberties Union (ACLU), an organization dedicated to protecting the rights and freedoms of U.S. citizens, vigorously protest the idea of defining violence as obscene. The ACLU points out that this could result in the banning of anything that has a violent theme, including paintings, novels, and plays that are considered masterpieces. "We're really concerned about extending the obscenity exception to violence," said Terri Schroder, an analyst with the ACLU. "Museums, libraries, schools, all sorts of institutions could really be in jeopardy."[63]

Media regulation at the local and state level

As soon as the MPAA film ratings system identified certain movies as inappropriate for children, many city and state lawmakers tried to codify the restrictions as law. Some states banned the showing of previews for R-rated features at G- and PG-rated movies. Legislators in Missouri proposed that minors be restricted from buying or renting videocassettes of R-rated films.

Similarly, once the RIAA established its Parental Advisory label, city councils passed ordinances and state legislators proposed laws to restrict children's access to albums carrying the label. By the early 1990s, many cities—including Memphis, Tennessee; San Antonio, Texas; and Jacksonville, Florida—had even passed laws banning minors from attending concerts that featured "potentially harmful" material. In 1998 South Carolina legislators proposed a bill establishing music concert ratings that would apply to the whole state.

More than twenty states proposed bills seeking to establish fines for retailers who sold music with Parental Advisory stickers to minors. Connecticut state senator John Kissel introduced similar legislation in 2001, explaining, "Many of these cassettes and CDs are replete with hate speech and calls to violence."[64]

Few of these efforts to legally restrict minors' access to R-rated films and Parental Advisory–labeled music became law, because the councils or legislatures considering the proposed bills thought they ran afoul of the U.S. Constitution. Laws that did pass were later overturned by the courts for the same reason.

Video game restrictions

As video games became more realistic and more violent, lawmakers across the nation took a much harder look at them. Soon there were numerous efforts to criminalize the sale and rental of violent video games to children, require government enforcement of ESRB ratings, and prevent the sale of games portraying violence against police officers. From 2000 to 2002, at least sixteen anti-video-game bills were introduced in states and cities across the nation.

In October 2000, St. Louis County Council member Jeff Wagener introduced an ordinance to restrict minors' access to violent video games in arcades. The law also criminalized the sale or display of violent video games to minors in stores. Once the ordinance passed, the video game trade group, the Interactive Digital Software Association, immediately challenged it as unconstitutional. "This is fundamentally . . . a case about the Constitutional status of video games and our belief that regulation of this sort doesn't pass Constitutional muster,"[65] said Doug Lowenstein, president of the IDSA.

The U.S. District Court judge hearing the case disagreed. He said that since video games do not communicate an idea, they cannot legally be considered "speech." And if they were not speech, they were not protected by the First Amendment.

The IDSA immediately appealed to a higher court, which in June 2003 overturned the previous ruling. According to the Eighth U.S. Circuit Court of Appeals, based in Chicago, video games are a form of speech and thus are protected by the Constitution. "Whether we believe the advent of violent video games adds anything of value to society is irrelevant; guided by the First Amendment, we are obliged to recognize that 'they are as much entitled to the protection of free speech as the best of literature,' "[66] the court said.

In May 2003 Washington became the first state to pass a

bill against video games. The law specifically targeted video or computer games depicting violence against law enforcement officials—so-called cop-killer games. Retailers selling such games to children under seventeen were subject to fines of up to $500.

The IDSA quickly filed a lawsuit to prevent enforcement of the Washington law. Other groups opposing the bill included the ACLU and the Media Coalition, which represents

Senator Sam Brownback opens a 1999 hearing on ways to stop the merchandising of violence to children. In the foreground is a promotional poster for a video game.

publishers, bookstores, librarians, and magazine distributors as well as recording and movie studios and video-game manufacturers and retailers. "Games are art," said Jason Della Rocca, program director of the International Game Developer Association, which also contested the law. "Games should be afforded the same sort of protection and respect as other forms of speech."[67] A hearing was scheduled for mid-2004, and until the case could be heard, a judge's preliminary injunction prevented the law from taking effect.

Meanwhile, additional states moved to place restrictions on violent video games. Assemblyman Leland Yee of California introduced a bill to restrict children from buying or renting first-person shooter video games. "This is all about saving our kids,"[68] Yee declared.

"Government should do more"

In the wake of the April 1999 Columbine shootings, the country seemed prepared more than ever to support regulation of violence in the media. In a CNN survey taken shortly after the incident, respondents were asked whether "the federal government should do more"[69] to regulate violence in various media, and the proportion of those saying yes ranged from about two-thirds to about one-half, depending on the particular medium: Internet, 65 percent; video games, 58 percent; television, 56 percent; movies, 49 percent; popular music, 48 percent. Stunned Americans called on federal lawmakers to do something to prevent youth violence.

Legislators responded by introducing numerous bills in the U.S. House of Representatives and Senate. One, introduced by Representative Henry Hyde of Illinois, would have banned retailers from selling to minors any movies, video games, or sound recordings that featured explicitly violent or sexual material. Similar legislation appeared in the Senate. A bill proposed by Senator Ernest Hollings of South Carolina would have limited the broadcasting of programs with violent content to hours when most children would not be watching. Senators John McCain of Arizona and Joseph Lieberman of Connecticut cowrote a bill that would have required content labels on video games, movie videos, and sound recordings; manufacturers whose products did not display a label, and retailers who did not enforce age restrictions, would receive substantial fines.

Despite widespread emotional support for these and similar bills, the legislation ultimately languished in Congress. First Amendment concerns convinced most legislators not to support their passage.

Appeal to Hollywood

Instead, several senators put together a statement calling on the entertainment industry to adopt voluntary minimum standards limiting excessive violence and sexual content in the media. "Media industry leaders, as responsible corporate citizens, should come together and voluntarily commit to reining in the toxic mix of sex and violence that has come to dominate so many of the products they produce and negatively affect our children today,"[70] said Senator McCain.

The senators' consensus statement was signed by many other prominent figures, including former presidents Jimmy Carter and Gerald Ford, and former generals Colin Powell and Norman Schwartzkopf. The Appeal to Hollywood, as the statement was called, appeared in newspapers nationwide in July 1999. Copies were sent to entertainment leaders and posted on a website that citizens were encouraged to sign. Many people viewed the appeal as a veiled threat that legislation would soon follow if the entertainment industry did not respond.

Undermining the ratings systems

In June 1999 President Clinton had requested, and the Senate had authorized, a study of the entertainment industry. Fifteen months later, in September 2000, the Federal Trade Commission report was released. Entitled *Marketing Violent Entertainment to Children: A Review of Self-Regulation and Industry Practices in the Motion Picture, Music Recording and Electronic Game Industries*, the FTC study severely reprimanded the movie, music, and video game industries alike. It was clear, the report said, that all were aggressively marketing products with violent content to young people and children—despite the fact that the industries' own ratings and

Hilary Rosen (right), head of the RIAA, and Jack Valenti, director of the MPAA, testify at a 2001 Senate hearing on media violence.

labeling systems were designed to limit such content to the appropriate age groups.

Although anyone under the age of seventeen was supposed to be barred from R-rated movies without a parent or guardian, for example, the motion picture industry was advertising R-rated films to young people. Commercials for these films ran on television during after-school hours and on shows with large teen audiences. Ads were placed in high school newspapers, youth magazines, and comic books. Movie trailers advertising R-rated movies were being shown to audiences at G- and PG-rated movies. The FTC study concluded that 80 percent of R-rated movies were being marketed to kids under seventeen.

The recording industry was rebuked for advertising music with violent lyrics to teens in youth magazines and on television. Of the fifty-five music recordings carrying the Parental Advisory label, the report said, all were being marketed to youth under seventeen. The FTC conducted a secret shopper survey in which young children attempted to purchase labeled music recordings. They were successful 85 percent of the time.

The report also found that video game manufacturers were specifically marketing Mature-rated games to underage children. In fact, of 118 M-rated games, nearly 70 percent were targeted to kids under seventeen. M-rated video games were also advertised in youth magazines. Unaccompanied children ages thirteen to sixteen were able to buy these games 85 percent of the time, the FTC found.

The FTC report scolded the entertainment media for undermining their own ratings and parental advisory systems, and for frustrating "parents' attempts to protect their children from inappropriate material."[71] The commission called on the entertainment industry to police its marketing and to enhance and enforce its self-regulatory codes. It also called on Congress to continue to monitor the issue.

Media Marketing Accountability Act

In response to the continuing frustration with the entertainment industry, Senator Joseph Lieberman proposed the Media Marketing Accountability Act (MMAA). The legislation would forbid companies from advertising adult-rated material to anyone under the age of seventeen, and it would make the Federal Trade Commission responsible for enforcement.

Executives from the music, motion picture, and video game industries were present at the congressional hearings on the bill, held in July 2001. Legislators scolded the music industry for not providing more information in its Parental Advisory label. Hilary Rosen, chief executive of the Recording Industry Association of America, answered that the industry did not plan to go beyond its current labeling system. "There are people in the music industry who think we have [already] gone too far," Rosen said. "I think we have reached the right balance. . . . Because the parental advisory label is overly broad, we think it can offer more protection, not less protection,"[72] she said.

During discussion of the proposed bill, film industry president Jack Valenti pointed out that the MPAA ratings system was a voluntary program. If the Media Marketing Accountability Act passed, producers who participated in the program would be punished, while those who did not submit their films for MPAA rating review could target young audiences without fear of punishment.

The FTC associate director of advertising practices, C. Lee Peeler, told lawmakers that rather than legislation, "the Commission continues to believe vigilant self-regulation is the best approach to fix the problem [to ensure parents have adequate information about violent content of movies, music and video games]."[73] Ultimately the MMAA did not receive enough support to pass.

Entertainment industry responses

In the absence of legal restrictions on the labeling and marketing of media products with violent content, the entertainment industry—as had happened before when controversy arose—sought to address the concerns of lawmakers and private citizens alike through the adoption of additional voluntary measures. In the film industry, for example, the MPAA adopted voluntary new guidelines recommending that theater owners not show trailers advertising films rated R for violence when G-rated films were screened; the same recommendation was made for trailers accompanying G-rated movies on videocassettes and DVDs. In addition, to help parents learn more about films' ratings, the MPAA established the website www.filmratings.com. "Not only will parents find a film's rating here, but also the reasons why a movie received a particular rating,"[74] explained Jack Valenti.

For its part, the RIAA—after initially rejecting criticism leveled at the music industry in the 2000 FTC report, and insisting that its music ratings system was working well—decided in 2001 to begin conducting nationwide merchandising campaigns, using posters, countertop displays, and magazine advertising, to educate store consumers about the Parental Advisory label. The following year the RIAA announced that additional text explaining the four-word advisory logo was to be placed on albums, stating, "The

Parental Advisory is a notice to consumers that recordings identified by this logo may contain strong language or depictions of violence, sex or substance abuse. Parental discretion is advised."[75] Labeled albums were to be identified as such in all consumer print, radio, and television advertising. The same guidelines were to apply for CDs, records, tapes, and digitally downloaded files (MP3) for sale at Internet websites.

The video game industry—which has been commended by the FTC and legislators for maintaining the most detailed ratings system of all the major media industries—further refined its labeling system in mid-2003. At that time the Entertainment Software Rating Board introduced four new rating descriptors and bolder labeling to draw attention to the information. The new descriptors were intended to help consumers better understand the kind of violence in a game. The four categories are cartoon violence (including incidents in which the victim is unharmed), fantasy violence (human and nonhuman characters), intense violence (graphic and realistic-looking), and sexual violence (rape or other violent sexual acts). In the fall of 2003, the ESRB also introduced a new education campaign to increase consumer awareness of its ratings system. The campaign—featuring the slogan "OK to Play?"—included public service announcements in national magazines and major newspapers. Store displays and advertising urged parents to make sure games were appropriate for their children before buying them. The campaign also informed consumers of the change to the M and AO icons, which were modified to show minimum recommended age.

Does self-regulation work?

Despite the voluntary measures adopted by the entertainment industry, critics charge that products with violent content can still find their way into the hands of children who are too young. Many people complain that the alphabet of ratings and labels across the various media is too confusing. They call for a uniform ratings system that would be applied to television programs, films, music

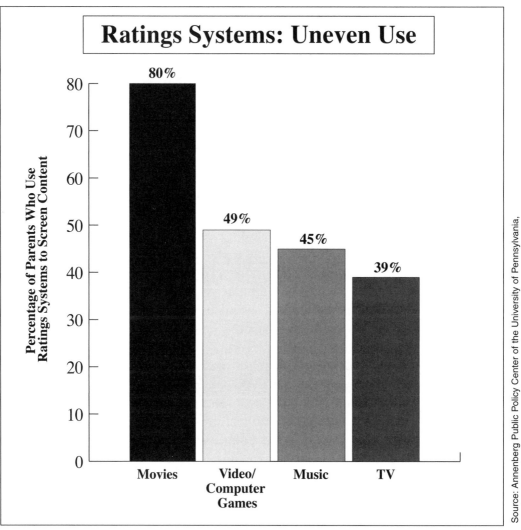

Ratings Systems: Uneven Use

Percentage of Parents Who Use Ratings Systems to Screen Content

- Movies: **80%**
- Video/Computer Games: **49%**
- Music: **45%**
- TV: **39%**

Source: Annenberg Public Policy Center of the University of Pennsylvania, Media in the Home 2000: The Fifth Annual Survey of Parents and Children.

recordings, and video and computer games. For now, however, the industries prefer to maintain their own systems, but they have created the Parental Media Guide website to better educate bewildered parents. The site (found at www.parentalguide.org) claims to provide "one-stop shopping" to each of these parental advisory systems.

But some critics question whether the entertainment industry is really doing all it can to help parents protect their children from inappropriate material. For example, in a report released in 2003, the Parents Television Council

(PTC) charged that advertisements for adult-rated material continue to air on shows popular with children. Ads for Eminem's *8 Mile* DVD, the report noted, ran on Fox's *American Idol*, which was the highest-rated show among children ages two to seventeen.

A PTC report released in June of 2002 had concluded that 30 percent of video game advertisements on TV ran from 8:00 P.M. to 9:00 P.M., informally considered the family hour. Advertisements for M-rated games repeatedly appeared during shows with large teen audiences. Another PTC study released in 2002 showed that one in four movie ads running during the family hour was for an R-rated film.

Suing the entertainment industry

In the absence of mandatory regulations or effective voluntary measures to keep inappropriate material away from children, some families of murder, suicide, and assault victims have brought lawsuits in an attempt to punish the entertainment industry and force it to make changes in its practices. The first such lawsuit, against the television networks CBS, NBC, and ABC, was filed in 1977 by the father of a fifteen-year-old Florida boy who had shot and killed an elderly neighbor. The suit, which claimed the teen had become desensitized to violence by watching six to eight hours of television a day, blamed crime shows such as *Kojak* for the murder.

Similarly, families of some young men who committed suicide have sought compensation from the music industry for their sons' deaths. In 1985 the parents of John McCollum sued Ozzy Osbourne for the nineteen-year-old's suicide. The suit blamed the song "Suicide Solution," claiming that its lyrics encouraged young people to take their lives as the answer to their personal problems. (For his part, Osbourne claimed that the song was about a friend who had died as the result of heavy drinking, and that it was intended as a warning against alcoholism.) British heavy metal band Judas Priest has also been sued by families who lost sons to suicide. Their deaths were blamed on lyrics in the 1978 album *Stained Class*.

The families of teenagers killed by Michael Carneal, shown here entering a courthouse in handcuffs, filed lawsuits holding media companies liable for the murders.

In 1999 the families of three teenage girls killed by school shooter Michael Carneal in West Paducah, Kentucky, filed lawsuits for $130 million against 24 media companies, seeking to hold them liable for the deaths. One of the entertainment products blamed was the 1995 movie *The Basketball Diaries*, starring Leonardo DiCaprio. It features a dream scene in which the main character guns down a teacher and school classmates. The lawsuit also blamed violent computer games. Games such as Quake made violence "pleasurable and attractive," the lawsuit stated, and they taught Carneal to point, shoot, and kill without regard for the "natural consequences."[76]

Families of students killed in the 1999 Columbine shootings also blamed the entertainment industry for creating a mindset of violence. In May 2001 several families of Columbine victims socked the entertainment industry with a $5 billion lawsuit. Twenty-five entertainment and video-game companies (including Sony Computer Entertainment and Nintendo of America) were targeted in a lawsuit alleging that shooters Dylan Klebold and Eric Harris had been influenced by media violence, particularly by the video game Doom II.

In none of these cases did the plaintiffs prevail, however, because the courts failed to find any direct evidence of causation. That is, it was not proved—in the estimation of the judges or juries hearing the various cases—that the deaths had been caused by the young killers' or suicide victims' listening to music with violent lyrics, watching violent movies or TV programs, or playing violent video games.

A continuing controversy

The debate over violence in the media has been going on for more than half a century. At certain times, the discussion seems largely confined to the pages of academic and professional journals, where researchers present and refute evidence from scientific studies and surveys. Periodically, however, the controversy seizes the attention of a wider audience, as details of a shooting spree or some other heinous act of violence committed by a troubled youth spill onto the front pages of newspapers and the covers of magazines and dominate the nightly news broadcasts. At those times Americans are left to consider what role violence in the media may have played in the most recent tragedy—and what, if anything, can or should be done to prevent a similar occurrence in the future.

Notes

Introduction

1. Quoted in Charles Feldman and Paul Vercammen, "Youth Violence Puts the Spotlight on Mass Media," CNN, March 26, 1998. www.cnn.com.

2. Gerard Jones, *Killing Monsters: Why Children Need Fantasy, Super Heroes, and Make-Believe Violence*. New York: Basic Books, 2002, p. 12.

3. Quoted in Mike Allen and Ellen Nakashima, "Clinton, Gore Hit Hollywood Marketing," *Washington Post,* September 12, 2000, p. A1.

Chapter 1: Violence in Film and Television

4. Stephen Prince, *Screening Violence*. New Brunswick, NJ: Rutgers University Press, 2003, p. 3.

5. "Death in the Media." *On the Media* (radio program), May, 2001. Transcript at www.wnyc.org.

6. Motion Picture Association of America (MPAA) website. www.mpaa.org.

7. MPAA website. www.mpaa.org.

8. MPAA website. www.mpaa.org.

9. MPAA website. www.mpaa.org.

10. Quoted in James D. Torr, ed., *Violence in the Media (Current Controversies)*. San Diego: Greenhaven, p. 13.

11. Quoted in Gina Kolata, "A Study Finds More Links Between TV and Violence," *New York Times*, March 29, 2002.

12. Quoted in Gloria DeGaetano, "Media Violence: Confronting the Issues and Taking Action." Media Literacy Review website. http://interact.uoregon.edu.

13. Quoted in FCC website, "V-Chip: Viewing Television Responsibly." www.fcc.gov.

14. Quoted in Alexandra Marks, "What Children See and Do: Studies of Violence on TV," *Christian Science Monitor.* April 17, 1998. http://search.csmonitor.com.

15. Quoted in D.A.R.E. America website, "Study: TV Violence Increasing," December 2003. www.dare.com.

16. Quoted in Eric Nuzum, *Parental Advisory: Music Censorship in America.* New York: Perennial, 2001, p. 18.

17. Quoted in Nuzum, *Parental Advisory,* p. 27.

18. Quoted in Nuzum. *Parental Advisory,* p. 31.

19. Quoted in Nuzum. *Parental Advisory,* p. 17.

20. Quoted in Nuzum. *Parental Advisory,* p. 54.

21. Recording Industry Association of America, "Parental Advisory." http://www.riaa.com.

22. Frank Palumbo, "Testimony Before the Senate Subcommittee on Oversight of Government Management, Restructuring, and the District of Columbia: The Social Impact of Music Violence," November 6, 1997. American Academy of Pediatrics. www.aap.org.

23. Palumbo, "Testimony Before the Senate Subcommittee." www.aap.org.

24. Palumbo, "Testimony Before the Senate Subcommittee." www.aap.org.

25. Quoted in Paul Duggan, "Shooter Pair Mixed Fantasy, Reality," *Washington Post*, April 22, 1999, p. A1.

26. Hilary Rosen, "Statement of Hilary Rosen, President and CEO, Recording Industry Association of America, Before the Committee on Governmental Affairs, 'Rating Entertainment Ratings,' " United States Senate, July 25, 2001. www.senate.gov.

27. Quoted in Lori O'Keefe, "Academy Supports Efforts to Loosen Grip of Media Violence on Children," *AAP News*, February 2001.

Chapter 3: Violence in Interactive Media

28. Quoted in Paul Keegan, "A Game Boy in the Cross Hairs," *New York Times,* May 23, 1999.

29. Dave Grossman and Gloria DeGaetano, *Stop Teaching Our Kids to Kill: A Call to Action Against TV, Movie and Video Game Violence.* New York: Crown Publishers, 1999, p. 4.

30. Quoted in Karen Wright, "Guns, Lies, and Video," *Discover*, April 2003.

31. Quoted in Duggan, "Shooter Pair Mixed Fantasy, Reality," p. A1.

32. Quoted in Janelle Brown, "Doom, Quake and Mass Murder," Salon.com, April 23, 1999.

33. Greg Costikyan, "Games Don't Kill People—Do They?" Salon.com, June 21, 1999.

34. Costikyan, "Games Don't Kill People."

35. Quoted in Richard Rhodes, "The Media-Violence Myth," *Rolling Stone*, November 23, 2000, p. 55.

36. Media Awareness Network, "Media Education and Media Violence." www.media-awareness.ca.

37. "Violent Video Games." Online News Hour, Public Broadcasting System, July 7, 2003. www.pbs.org.

38. Senator Lieberman Press Office, "Lieberman Says Kids Still Vulnerable to Violent Video Games, Calls for New Hearings on Kids' Access to Adult Materials," December 19, 2002. www.senate.gov.

39. Quoted in Brad Wright, "Sounding the Alarm on Video Game Ratings, CNN, December 20, 2002.

40. Eighth Annual MediaWise Video Game Report Card, December 2003. www.mediafamily.org.

41. National Public Radio, NPR/Kaiser/Kennedy School Poll: Kids & Technology Survey, 2000. www.npr.org.

Chapter 4: Linking Media Violence with Real-Life Violence

42. American Psychiatric Association, "Psychiatric Effects of Media Violence," 2003. www.psych.org.

43. Grossman and DeGaetano, *Stop Teaching Our Kids to Kill,* p. 33.

44. "Violent Media Is Good for Kids," Mother Jones.com Commentary, July 30, 2000. www.motherjones.com.

45. Rhodes, "The Media-Violence Myth," p. 55.

46. Geoffrey Cowley, "Why Children Turn Violent," *Newsweek*, April 6, 1998, p. 24.

47. Quoted in *Developmental Psychology,* March 2003.

48. Quoted in Rea Blakey, "Study Links TV Viewing Among Kids to Later Violence," CNN, March 28, 2002. www.cnn.com.

49. Craig A. Anderson and Karen E. Dill, "Video Games and Aggressive Thoughts, Feelings, and Behavior in the Laboratory and in Life," *Journal of Personality and Social Psychology* 78, 4 (2000): pp. 772–790.

50. Anderson and Dill, "Video Games and Aggressive Thoughts," pp. 772–790.

51. Richard Rhodes, "Hollow Claims About Fantasy Violence," *New York Times,* September 17, 2000.

52. Quoted in Wright, "Guns, Lies, and Video."

53. Rowell Huesmann and Leonard Eron, "Rhodes Is Careening Down the Wrong Road," American Booksellers for Free Expression. www.abffe.com.

54. "Joint Statement on the Impact of Entertainment Violence on Children," Congressional Public Health Summit, July 26, 2000. www.lionlamb.org.

55. Quoted in Diana Zuckerman, "What Is to Blame for Youth Violence?: The Media, Guns, Parenting, Poverty, Bad Programs, Or…" *Youth Today*, March 2001.

56. Quoted in Media Awareness Network, "Media Violence Debates." www.media-awareness.ca.

57. Quoted in National Coalition Against Censorship, "The First Amendment, Pop Culture and the Silly Season." www.ncac.org.

58. Quoted in Tom Jackman, "Escape 'The Matrix,' Go Directly to Jail: Some Defendants in Slaying Cases Make Reference to Hit Movie," *Washington Post,* March 17, 2003.

59. Free Expression Policy Project. www.fepproject.org.

60. Quoted in "Report Downplays Media-Violence Link," *American Family Association Journal*, March 2001. www.afa.net.

61. Quoted in "Report Downplays Media-Violence Link." www.afa.net.

Chapter 5: Regulating the Media

62. Quoted in Nat Hentoff, "NBC and the Government's Enforcers," *Washington Post*, October 18, 1997, p. A23.

63. Quoted in *American Libraries*, "News Briefs for June 14, 1999. http://archive.ala.org.

64. Quoted in "Parental Advisory: Music Censorship in America." http://ericnuzum.com.

65. Quoted in Mark Jurkowitz, "Appeals Court Holds Key in Battle over Regulation of Violent Video Games," *Boston Globe,* October 2, 2002, p. D1.

66. Quoted in John P. Mello Jr., "Video Game Violence Leads to Florida Law, *TechNews World*, January 20, 2004.

67. Quoted in Chris Morris, "Washington Bans "Violent" Game Sales," CNN, May 21, 2003. http://money.cnn.com.

68. Quoted in Jonathan Dee, "Playing Mogul," *New York Times*, December 21, 2003.

69. Keating Holland, "Poll: Violence in the Media Should Be Regulated," CNN, May 3, 1999. www.cnn.com.

70. Senator John McCain press release, "McCain Urges

Hollywood to Voluntarily Limit Media Violence," July 21, 1999. http://mccain.senate.gov.

71. Federal Trade Commission, *Marketing Violent Entertainment to Children: A Review of Self-Regulation and Industry Practices in the Motion Picture, Music Recording & Electronic Game Industries*. September 2000.

72. Quoted in Nicole C. Wong, "Panel Faults Music Labels: Warning Are Vague, Lawmakers Say," *Washington Post*, July 21, 2001, p. E1.

73. Quoted in Wong, "Panel Faults Music Labels," p. E1.

74. "Valenti Testifies in Congress on Industry's Commitment to Reduce Children's Exposure to Violent Content," July 20, 2001, press release. www.mpaa.org.

75. RIAA, "Parental Advisory." www.riaa.com.

76. Quoted in Sandy Brundage, "Blood and Thunder." www.gamers.com.

Glossary

aggression: Physical or verbal behavior that is intended to harm another person.

antisocial: Showing behavior or attitudes that go against the values of general society or authority.

assault: A violent physical attack; a threat or attempt to inflict bodily harm on a person.

censorship: The act of examining and removing parts considered objectionable from a work, such as words from a book or scenes from a film or television program.

control group: A group that receives standard treatment or no intervention in a research study.

first-person shooter game: A video game in which the player controls the game and experiences the action through the eyes of the main character, whose task is to shoot and kill opponents.

homicide: The killing of one human being by another.

PCA: Production Code Administration, an internal film censorship agency from the 1930s to 1950s.

prime time: Hours when television is watched the most, typically between 8 P.M. and 10 P.M.

rape: A violent crime involving forced sexual intercourse.

sadomasochism: The desire to receive pain and inflict it on others.

squibs: Red-dye capsules, wired to explode on cue, that are used by filmmakers to simulate gunshot wounds on victims' bodies.

suicide: The act of deliberately killing oneself.

ultraviolent: Extremely violent; containing a large amount of violent content.

Organizations to Contact

American Academy of Pediatrics (AAP)

141 Northwest Point Blvd.
Elk Grove Village, IL 60009-0927
(847) 981-7873
www.aap.org

Through its educational campaign Media Matters, the AAP works to educate children, parents, teachers, and pediatricians about the impact that the media can have on behavior and lifestyle choices affecting the health of young people. Information on studies linking aggressive behavior with heavy media use and on media education can be found at the AAP website.

Center for Media Literacy

4727 Wilshire Blvd., Suite 403
Los Angeles, CA 90010
(800) 226-9494
fax: (323) 931-4474
www.medialit.org

The nonprofit organization Center for Media Literacy develops educational programs and materials to encourage critical thinking about all types of mass media. CML also conducts workshops, national conferences, teacher training, and seminars on promoting critical thinking about the media.

Federal Communications Commission

Mass Media Bureau
Complaints/Enforcement Division

Political Programming Branch, Room 3443
445 12th St. SW
Washington, DC 20554
(202) 418-1430
www.fcc.gov

The federal agency that oversees the policies and licensing of programs related to the electronic media, the FCC provides information on the V-chip and is a source for copies of the FTC reports on marketing violent entertainment to children.

Free Expression Policy Project

275 Seventh Ave., 9th Floor
New York, NY 10001
(212) 807-6222 ext. 12
fax: (212) 807-6245
www.fepproject.org

A think tank on artistic and intellectual freedom, the Free Expression Policy Project provides research and analysis of censorship issues. Concerned that filters and ratings systems restrict access to information, the organization supports the concept of media literacy as an alternative to censorship. The website provides information on media violence and links to other sources.

Killology Research Group

P.O. Box 9280
Jonesboro, AR 72403
(870) 931-5172
www.killology.com

The Killology Research Group "focuses on the reactions of healthy people in killing circumstances (such as police and military in combat) and the factors that enable and restrain killing in these situations." A firm believer that violent media causes the desensitization needed to create killers, Lt. Col. Dave Grossman founded the organization, which provides counseling and speakers. The website provides links to media violence initiatives.

The Lion & Lamb Project
4300 Montgomery Ave., Suite 104
Bethesda, MD 20814
(301) 654-3091
fax : 301-654-2394
e-mail: lionlamb@lionlamb.org
www.lionlamb.org

This nonprofit organization works to stop the marketing of violence to children, and to educate parents and other concerned adults about the need to reduce the demand for violent entertainment products. Besides providing informational resources, the Lion & Lamb Project sponsors workshops, holds press conferences, and contributes to congressional testimony on media violence.

Media Awareness Network
1500 Merivale Rd., 3rd Floor
Ottawa, Ontario
Canada K2E 6Z5
(613) 224-7721
fax: (613) 224-1958
e-mail: info@media-awareness.ca
www.media-awareness.ca

Through a website written in English and French, this Canadian organization offers resources and support for those interested in media and information literacy for young people. Issues covered include media violence and stereotyping.

Mediascope, Inc.
100 Universal City Plaza, Bldg. 6159
Universal City, CA 91608
(818) 733-3180
fax: (818) 733-3181
e-mail: facts@mediascope.org
www.mediascope.org

The nonprofit organization Mediascope seeks to work with the entertainment industry to encourage responsible portrayals in television, film, the Internet, video games, music, and advertising. To raise awareness of issues, the organization sponsors studies of media issues, such as the influence of ratings on children's media choices, and analyzes violent content in television and film.

MediaWatch

517 Wellington St. West, Suite 204
Toronto, ON
Canada M5V 1G1
(416) 408-2065
www.mediawatch.ca

A nonprofit organization, MediaWatch works to eliminate sexism in the media and to challenge biased stereotypes portrayed in the media. It sponsors research on media issues and provides informational videos, media literacy information, and newsletters to educate the consumers of mass media and the media industries.

National Institute on Media and the Family (NIMF)

606 24th Ave. South, Suite 606
Minneapolis, MN 55454
(888) 672-5437
fax: (612)-672-4113
www.mediafamily.org

The nonprofit National Institute on Media and the Family provides information and educational materials on the impact of the media on children and families. The organization features a yearly MediaWise Video Game Report Card and provides other resources on evaluating media.

National PTA

330 N. Wabash Ave., Suite 2100
Chicago, IL 60611
(800) 307-4782
Fax: (312) 670-6783
www.pta.org

In conjunction with the National Cable Television Association and Cable in the Classroom, the National PTA offers a pamphlet entitled "Taking Charge of Your TV," as well as other educational information for fostering good television habits and understanding the impact of the medium.

Parents Television Council (PTC)

707 Wilshire Blvd. #2075
Los Angeles, CA 90017
(213) 629-9255
www.ParentsTV.org

In an effort to make television socially responsible, the PTC tracks objectionable content on broadcast TV programming and provides the results in in-depth reports and analyses. Past studies have focused on inappropriate content featured during the "family hour" and the television ratings system.

For Further Reading

Books

Dave Grossman and Gloria DeGaetano, *Stop Teaching Our Kids to Kill: A Call to Action Against TV, Movie and Video Game Violence*. New York: Crown Publishers, 1999. Accuses the media of conditioning children to be violent and—in the case of video games—actually teaching them shooting skills. Provides background information on studies supporting a link between media violence and real-life violence.

Gerard Jones, *Killing Monsters: Why Children Need Fantasy, Super Heroes, and Make-Believe Violence*. New York: Basic Books, 2002. Defends the presence of violence in the media, asserting that make-believe violence is a necessary part of growing up.

Eric D. Nuzum, *Parental Advisory: Music Censorship in America*. New York: Perennial, 2001. An overview of the history of rock and roll music and how it has been challenged, suppressed, legislated, and banned in the United States.

James D. Torr, ed., *Violence in Film and Television (Examining Pop Culture)*. San Diego: Greenhaven Press, 2002. Provides a selection of essays dealing with violence in the media, including films, TV shows, and video games.

Websites

ESRB—Entertainment Software Rating Board (www.esrb.org). This website offers definitions of the rating symbols and content descriptors with which the video game industry labels its products. The site also provides a search tool enabling users to find the ratings of specific games.

Movie Ratings (www.mpaa.org/movieratings). On this website, sponsored by the Motion Picture Association of America, users can search a database for the rating of a particular film.

Parental Media Guide (www.parentalguide.org). This website seeks to provide parents and caregivers with a central resource for accessing information on the ratings systems of the film, TV, recording, and video and computer game industries. It is sponsored by the Entertainment Software Rating Board, Motion Picture Association of America, National Association of Broadcasters, National Cable & Telecommunications Association, Recording Industry Association of America, and TV Parental Guidelines.

Works Consulted

Books

Sissela Bok, *Mayhem: Violence as Public Entertainment.* Reading, MA: Addison-Wesley, 1998. A prominent philosopher examines the social implications of violence in the entertainment media.

William Dudley, ed., *Media Violence: Opposing Viewpoints.* San Diego: Greenhaven Press, 1999. This collection presents a wide range of perspectives—from scholars, media critics, child health advocates, lawyers, and politicians, among others—on various aspects of the media violence debate.

Jeffrey Goldstein, ed., *Why We Watch: The Attractions of Violent Entertainment.* New York: Oxford University Press, 1998. A collection of essays focusing on the reasons violent entertainment is so popular in contemporary America.

Dave Grossman and Gloria DeGaetano, *Stop Teaching Our Kids to Kill: A Call to Action Against TV, Movie and Video Game Violence.* New York: Crown Publishers, 1999. A retired U.S. Army lieutenant colonel and his coauthor make the case that media violence is akin to military basic training in preparing children to kill.

Gerard Jones, *Killing Monsters: Why Children Need Fantasy, Super Heroes, and Make-Believe Violence.* New York: Basic Books, 2002. Jones, a comic-book writer, argues that fantasy violence is actually good for children, by helping them to work through their anger in a nondestructive way.

Newton Minow, *Abandoned in the Wasteland: Children, Television, and the First Amendment.* New York: Hill and Wang, 1995. As chair of the Federal Communications

Commission in the early 1960s, Minow characterized American TV as a "vast wasteland." In this book he argues that broadcasters are still failing the nation's children—and that they hide behind the First Amendment whenever calls for reform are heard.

Eric Nuzum, *Parental Advisory: Music Censorship in America*. New York: Perennial, 2001. In this highly readable volume, a pop-culture critic examines the history of attempts to keep "inappropriate" songs from the ears of children.

Stephen Prince, ed., *Screening Violence*. New Brunswick, NJ: Rutgers University Press, 2003. Essays on the history and effects of cinematic violence.

James D. Torr, ed., *Violence in the Media: Current Controversies*. San Diego: Greenhaven Press, 2002. How serious is the problem of violence in the media? Does violence in the media make children and teenagers more violent? Experts weigh in on these and other important questions.

Marie Winn, *The Plug-In Drug: Television, Computers, and Family Life*. New York: Penguin, 2002. The author examines the toll television viewing and computer gaming take on the imagination and school achievement of children, and she offers suggestions for breaking dependence on electronic entertainment.

Periodicals

Mike Allen and Ellen Nakashima, "Clinton, Gore Hit Hollywood Marketing Ads Aimed at Kids: Could Spur Rules, Industry Is Told," *Washington Post*, September 12, 2000.

Craig A. Anderson and Brad J. Bushman, "The Effects of Media Violence on Society," *Science*, March 2002.

Craig A. Anderson and Karen E. Dill, "Video Games and Aggressive Thoughts, Feelings, and Behavior in the Laboratory and in Life," *Journal of Personality and Social Psychology* (vol. 78, no. 4), 2000.

Craig Anderson, Nicholas L. Carnagey, and Janie Eubanks, "Exposure to Violent Media: The Effects of Songs with Violent Lyrics on Aggressive Thoughts and Feelings," *Journal of Personality and Social Psychology* (vol. 84, no. 5), 2003.

Geoffrey Cowley, "Why Children Turn Violent," *Newsweek*, April 6, 1998.

Eric Danton, "Study Links Music Lyrics with Violent Behavior," *Hartford Courant*, May 7, 2003.

Jonathan Dee, "Playing Mogul," *New York Times*, December 21, 2003.

Paul Duggan, "Shooter Pair Mixed Fantasy, Reality," *Washington Post*, April 22, 1999.

"The Fight over Violence," *Scholastic Scope*, November 15, 2002.

Nat Hentoff, "NBC and the Government's Enforcers," *Washington Post*, October 18, 1997.

Bill Holland, "Does RIAA Labeling System Work?" *Billboard*, September 23, 2000.

Tom Jackman, "Escape 'The Matrix,' Go Directly to Jail: Some Defendants in Slaying Cases Make Reference to Hit Movie," *Washington Post*, March 17, 2003.

Mark Jurkowitz, "Appeals Court Holds Key in Battle over Regulation of Violent Video Games," *Boston Globe*, October 2, 2002.

Paul Keegan, "A Game Boy in the Cross Hairs," *New York Times*, May 23, 1999.

———, "Culture Quake," *Mother Jones*, November/ December 1999.

Louise Kennedy, "The Rating Game," *Boston Globe*, June 30, 2002.

Gina Kolata, "A Study Finds More Links Between TV and Violence," *New York Times*, March 29, 2002.

Daphne Lavers, "The Verdict on Media Violence: It's Ugly . . . and Getting Uglier," *Insight on the News*, May 13, 2002.

Michael Medved, "That's Entertainment?" *National Interest*, Summer 2002.

Michael Craig Miller, "Does Violence in the Media Cause Violent Behavior?" *Harvard Mental Health Letter*, September 2001.

S. A. Miller, "Malvo Team Cites Role of Violent Media," *Washington Times*. December 8, 2003.

Constance Faye Mudore, "Does TV Violence Kill?" *Current Health*, February 2000.

Liza Mundy, "Do You Know Where Your Children Are?" *Washington Post*, November 16, 2003.

Joseph Pereira, "Just How Far Does First Amendment Protection Go?" *Wall Street Journal*, January 10, 2003.

Rhoda Rabkin, "Children, Entertainment, and Marketing, *Consumers' Research Magazine*, June 2002.

Tony Reichhardt, "Playing with Fire?" *Nature*, July 24, 2003.

Richard Rhodes, "Hollow Claims About Fantasy Violence," *New York Times*, September 17, 2000.

———, "The Media-Violence Myth," *Rolling Stone*, November 23, 2000.

Christopher Stern, "Explicit Songs Still Marketed to Children," *Washington Post*, April 25, 2001.

"Violent TV, Movies, Make Kids Meaner to Each Other," *Nation's Health*, October 2002.

Nicole Wong, "Panel Faults Music Labels: Warnings Are Vague, Lawmakers Say," *Washington Post*, July 21, 2001.

Karen Wright, "Guns, Lies, and Video," *Discover*, April 2003.

Diana Zuckerman, "What Is to Blame for Youth Violence?: The Media, Guns, Parenting, Poverty, Bad Programs, Or…" *Youth Today*, March 2001.

Internet Sources

American Academy of Pediatrics, "Some Things You Should Know About Media Violence and Media Literacy." www.aap.org.

American Academy of Pediatrics Committee on Public Education, "Media Violence" (Policy Statement). *Pediatrics*, November 2001. http://aappolicy.aappublications.org.

American Family Association, "Report Downplays Media-Violence Link," *American Family Association Journal*, March 2001. www.afa.net.

American Library Association, "News Briefs for June 14, 1999. *American Libraries*. http://archive.ala.org.

American Psychological Association, "Violence on Television—What Do Children Learn? What Can Parents Do?" www.apa.org.

Tustin Amole, "Where to Place the Blame?" *Denver Rocky Mountain News*, April 20, 1999. http://denver.rockymountainnews.com.

Craig A. Anderson, "Violent Video Games Increase Aggression and Violence," Testimony at the Senate Commerce Committee Hearing on the Impact of Interactive Violence on Children, March 21, 2000. www.psychology.iastate.edu.

Chris Black, Gene Randall, and the Associated Press. "White House Summit Looks for Answers to Youth Violence." CNN. May 10, 1999. www.cnn.com.

Rea Blakely, "Study Links TV Viewing Among Kids to Later Violence." CNN. March 28, 2002. www.cnn.com.

Janelle Brown, "Doom, Quake and Mass Murder," Salon.com. April 23, 1999. www.salon.com.

Sandy Brundage, "Blood and Thunder." Gamers.com. www.gamers.com.

CNN, "Laura Bush Opens New Chapter with Russia," December 31, 2003. www.cnn.com.

———, "Florida City Aims to Curb Violent Video Games," January 19, 2004. www.cnn.com.

———, "Record Warning Labels Under Fire in Senate," June 17, 1998. www.cnn.com.

Congressional Public Health Summit, "Joint Statement on the Impact of Entertainment Violence on Children," July 26, 2000. www.lionlamb.org.

Greg Costikyan, "Games Don't Kill People—Do They?" Salon.com. June 21, 1999. www.salon.com.

"Death in the Media," *On the Media* (radio program), May 5, 2001. www.wnyc.org.

Entertainment Software Association, "Computer and Video Game Software Sales Break $7 Billion in 2003." www.theesa.com.

Entertainment Software Rating Board, "ESRB Game Ratings." www.theesa.com.

Federal Trade Commission: Commission and Staff Reports, "Marketing Violent Entertainment to Children," June 2002, December 2001, April 2001, September 2000. www.ftc.gov.

Gloria DeGaetano, "Media Violence: Confronting the Issues and Taking Action," *Media Literacy Review*. http://interact.uoregon.edu.

Charles Feldman and Paul Vercammen, "Youth Violence Puts the Spotlight on Mass Media," CNN Interactive, March 26, 1998. www.cnn.com.

Free Expression Policy Project, "Fact Sheets: Media Violence." www.fepproject.org.

———, "Issue: Violence in the Media." www.fepproject.org.

Manny Frishberg, "Video-Game Merchants Under Fire," *Wired*, April 30, 2003. www.wired.com.

Helen Gerosthathos, "Media Violence and the First Amendment: The Conflict Between Freedom of Speech and Protecting America's Youth," Center for First Amendment Rights. www.cfarfreedom.org.

Keating Holland, "Poll: Violence in the Media Should Be Regulated," CNN, May 3, 1999. www.cnn.com.

Kaiser Family Foundation, "Few Parents Use V-Chip to Block TV Sex and Violence, but More Than Half Use TV Ratings to Pick What Kids Can Watch." www.kff.org.

Brad King, "Wanna Play Doom? Not in St. Louis," *Wired*. September 30, 2002. www.wired.com.

"Lieberman Says Kids Still Vulnerable to Violent Video Games, Calls for New Hearings on Kids' Access to Adult Materials," Senator Joseph Lieberman's Press Office, December 19, 2002. www.senate.gov.

Lion & Lamb Project, "Media Violence." www.lionlamb.org.

Alexandra Marks, "What Children See and Do: Studies of Violence on TV," *Christian Science Monitor*, April 17, 1998. http://search.csmonitor.com.

"McCain Urges Hollywood to Voluntarily Limit Media Violence," Senator John McCain's Press Office, July 21, 1999. http://mccain.senate.gov.

Media Awareness Network, "The Business of Media Violence." www.media-awareness.ca.

———, "Media Education and Media Violence." www.media-awareness.ca.

John P. Mello Jr., "Video Game Violence Leads to Florida Law, *TechNewsWorld*, January 20, 2004. www.technewsworld.com.

Chris Morris, "Washington Bans 'Violent' Game Sales," CNN, May 21, 2003. http://money.cnn.com.

Motion Picture Association of America, "Movie Rating: How It Works." www.mpaa.org.

National Coalition Against Censorship, "The First Amendment, Pop Culture and the Silly Season." www.ncac.org.

National Institute on Media and the Family, "Fact Sheet: Children and Media Violence." www.mediafamily.org.

———, "Fact Sheet: Effects of Video Game Playing on Children." www.mediafamily.org.

———, "Fact Sheet: History of Television." www.mediafamily.org.

———, "Fact Sheet: Music and Children." www.mediafamily.org.

———, "Fact Sheet: MTV." www.mediafamily.org.

———, "MediaWise Video Game Report Card," December 2003. www.mediafamily.org.

National Public Radio Online, "Survey Shows Widespread Enthusiasm for High Technology," February–March 2000. www.npr.org.

Lori O'Keefe, "Academy Supports Efforts to Loosen Grip of Media Violence on Children," *AAP News*, February 2001. www.aap.org.

"Parental Media Guide." www.parentalguide.org.

Parents Television Council, "Kids in the Crosshairs: Children Still Targeted in Marketing of Adult Rated Entertainment." www.parentstv.org.

———, "TV Bloodbath: Violence on Prime Time Broadcast TV." www.parentstv.org.

Recording Industry Association of America, "Parental Advisory." www.riaa.com.

Mark Sappenfield, "Mounting Evidence Links TV Viewing to Violence," *Christian Science Monitor*, March 29, 2002. www.csmonitor.com.

"Violent Video Games," *News Hour with Jim Lehrer*, July 7, 2003. www.pbs.org.

Brad Wright, "Sounding the Alarm on Video Game Ratings," CNN, December 20, 2002. www.cnn.com.

Index

Picture Credits

444

About the Author

LeeAnne Gelletly is a freelance writer and editor living outside Philadelphia, Pennsylvania. She has worked in publishing for more than twenty years.